YOUR BEST YEAR 2018

by lisa jacobs

"The brick walls are there for a reason. The brick walls are not there to keep us out. The brick walls are there to give us a chance to show how badly we want something. [The] brick walls are there to stop the people who don't want it badly enough. They're there to stop the other people."—Randy Pausch

Cover Art: Tomas Veselovsky
Cover Design: Jennie Rensink

Your Best Year 2018
Copyright © 2018 by Lisa Jacobs. All rights reserved.

Limit of Liability: While the author has used her best efforts in preparing this book, she makes no representations or warranties in respect to the contents and specifically disclaims any implied fitness for a particular purpose. The advice and strategies contained herein may not be suitable for your situation. Consult with a professional where appropriate. The author shall not be liable for any loss of profit or any other commercial damages.

For more information or bulk sales requests, please visit marketyourcreativity.com to contact the author directly.

Book Objective: Achieve what you want while reducing time-wasting errors, habits, and busywork. Create a more efficient routine and improve focus. Clarify what is vague and ambiguous about your goals, actions, and fears.

TABLE OF CONTENTS

HOW TO USE THIS WORKBOOK

I have lofty goals for this workbook. I want you to find and embrace unlimited potential. I want you to accomplish *whatever it is* you set out to do for the betterment of your life and business. I want you to obliterate time-wasting inefficiencies, mindless busywork, and bad habits.

I want you to leave this book feeling motivated and empowered, get an edge over the competition, and dominate your industry. You are 100% in charge of the results you create.

I want you to be so proud of yourself—for all that you accomplish in the coming year—that dignity radiates from your core. You've already got it in you. Let's give it LIFE!

Before we get started, I want to provide you with an overview of all we're going to cover in this book. For the last five years, I've been intensely studying human behavior and personal achievement at an average *four hundred* hours per year. In the last two years, I shattered limitations that had been keeping me stuck all my life.

I'm Lisa Jacobs, a radical advocate for growth and change. I've worked with thousands of online entrepreneurs to help them improve focus and efficiency in their businesses. I've taken hundreds of business owners from a state of uncertainty to top-selling industry leaders. I've mentored powerful women on their way to seven-figure salaries. I'm the real deal, and if this is the first year you're finding this workbook (in its fifth edition), you're in for a real treat.

You're about to have the year of your life, and I have great news: you already have all of the resources you need to succeed (without buying another book, taking another training session, or earning another certificate). You are enough, you have enough, and you offer enough to make all of your entrepreneurial dreams come true.

And I should know, I turned a few simple ideas into a thriving online business that's earned more than half a million dollars in the last two years. While I've always had an entrepreneurial spirit, I haven't always known how to be a *successful* entrepreneur. This book takes my proven systems and methods, and shows you the way.

Now that I've finally mastered the basics, I won't sugarcoat them for you. You won't see success overnight. The need for instant gratification will be your downfall. There are no get-rich-easy schemes or magic bullets. A sense of entitlement will be your demise.

In order to have a breakthrough year, you have to throw the idea that everything magically works out, out the window. And that's coming from a believer in the law of attraction, crystal attributes, affirmations, and oracle cards. Positive thinking doesn't work until you do!

Right from the kickoff of *Your Best Year 2018*, I'm going to speak to the next level YOU. I want to appeal to her, strengthen her, and help you bring her to life. It's your time, and you're going to take it to the next level this year. It's going to be *hard work*. At times, you'll suffer discomfort (and that's okay, you'll survive). If, and only IF you agree to learn, adapt, evolve, and endure, you will *thrive*. You'll reach peaks of personal achievement you never thought possible.

Not only do you have all the resources you need to succeed, you also have all the answers. You have enough *and* you know enough—right now, before we even begin! You already know what you need to do next, that little nugget is nagging at you from somewhere within the recesses of your subconscious.

Maybe it's saying …

- write that book, or
- open my own storefront, or
- start a blog, or
- create that video series, or
- upgrade my marketing system, or
- hire a professional photographer, or
- finally go learn *that thing* I've always wanted to try.

Or maybe your list is much more specific, as mine has been this year: find a trustworthy financial advisor well-versed in tax advantages for online business, find a reliable host for live streaming video to a large audience, and find a web developer that can eliminate as many third-parties as possible so I can take back control and deliverability of my presentations.

You already know whatever it is you need to do to breakthrough to the next level this year. It's cozily tucked away under a warm comfort zone of a blanket. You're not wondering what you'll do, but rather, *how in the world you'll do it all*. Where do you even begin to tackle that beast? What are his weak points? How do you take the first bite? How long does it even take to eat something that size? Worse, it always feels as though you're going into the battle blind!

Your Best Year 2018 is here to show you the way. It will help you tackle the next level beast, but I won't pussyfoot around the challenge ahead. That would be a disservice to us both. This book will require you to acknowledge your strengths and stop babying your weaknesses. Being subtle about your accomplishments won't help you showcase them, and avoiding your pain points will only prolong them.

I want you to be brutally honest with yourself. On a scale of 1 to 10, how **committed** have you been to making your business work thus far? The majority of clients I ask register at about a 7, but upon closer examination on my part, we bring their *real answer* down to a 5.

On a scale of 1 to 10, how **focused** have your work hours been to date? In other words, how much time do you spend on growth and profit, and how much time do you spend on busywork and unnecessary fluff? The majority of my clients generously give themselves a 6, but I'd bring most people's answers down to a 4, at best.

On average, most online business owners are 50% committed and 40% focused.

What would happen if you came into 2018 fully committed with a Mad Max focus on the work that matters and the results you want? What would happen if you gave 100%? I'll tell you what! You would make your most aspirational goals come true.

You would finally make the changes in your life you've been meaning to make all these years. You'd produce the results you've always craved. You'd feel satisfied and fulfilled. You would feel so *proud*. You'd feel worthy and deserving of the success you have worked so hard to achieve. You would feel powerful and in charge of your destiny.

The truth is, most business owners know exactly what they need to do next in order to grow their businesses, but they fail to do so. Whether it's a rebrand, professional services, virtual assistance, web development, product development, email marketing, or quality lead generation—there's probably a list of things you KNOW you need to do to get to the next level, you're just not taking the leap.

The vast internet in which we do business is as scary and unforgiving as the mighty jungle. It is easy to get lost. You'll feel overwhelmed and outmaneuvered. It's easy to panic. You might get eaten alive, and there's a very high probability of failure.

That's why, in *Your Best Year 2018*, I will teach you lessons of survival and endurance.

Survival is an act of bull-headed determination, in spite of difficult circumstances. When you come into this game, your odds of winning are 90/10. With only a 10% chance of making it out on top, the deck is heavily stacked against you. If that's not a game of survival, I don't know what is!

So, I studied survival in life and death situations, and I noticed a common theme amongst people who'd made it against all odds. Each one had described the mental breakdowns and panic they faced as the impeding threats closed in around them. Each had different coping methods and techniques. It was as much a matter of endurance as it was one of survival.

Endurance is a long-term strategy for survival. To endure, you need to be mentally fit, you need to have a reason to fight, and your endeavors need to be championed by those closest to you. Endurance means to give all you've got, keep your cool, push your breaking point, and barrel forward no matter what. You must be 100% committed to the finish line.

"IF YOU WANT TO TAKE THE ISLAND, BURN THE BOATS."—Julius Caesar

With this book, I want you to become an unstoppable, relentless force toward your own good. Have a pen handy. *Your Best Year 2018* is meant to be worked through, scribbled in, and answered right on the page, while you're thinking of it.

This book is a monster, hungry for your obstacles and starved for your achievement. Are you ready to feed it?

YOUR BEST YEAR IS HERE

This workbook contains dozens of exercises arranged into thoughtfully planned sections to help you make the most of the upcoming calendar year. At the start of the book, we'll discuss what it *really takes* to reach your goals in online business and beyond. You'll find new ideas on survival and endurance that will help you get your mind right for the battle ahead.

First, you'll assess the current status of your business and what you're up against. Find these exercises in chapters, "State of the Union" and "Survey the Land." These will help you measure the distance between where you are and where you want to be.

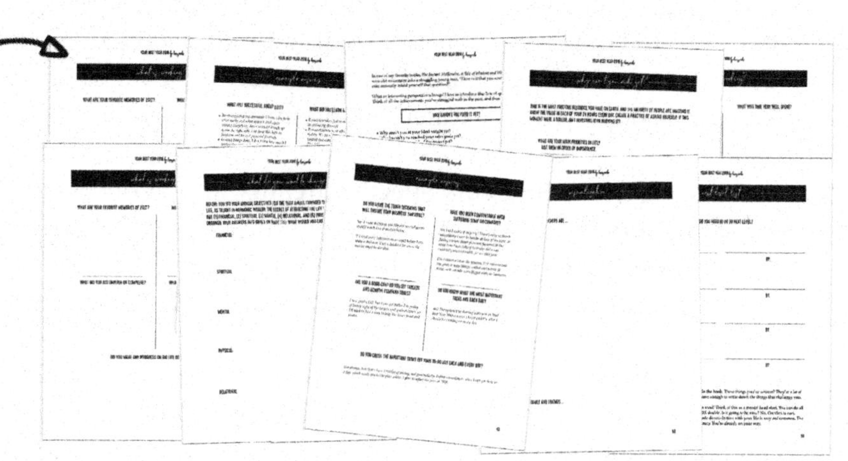

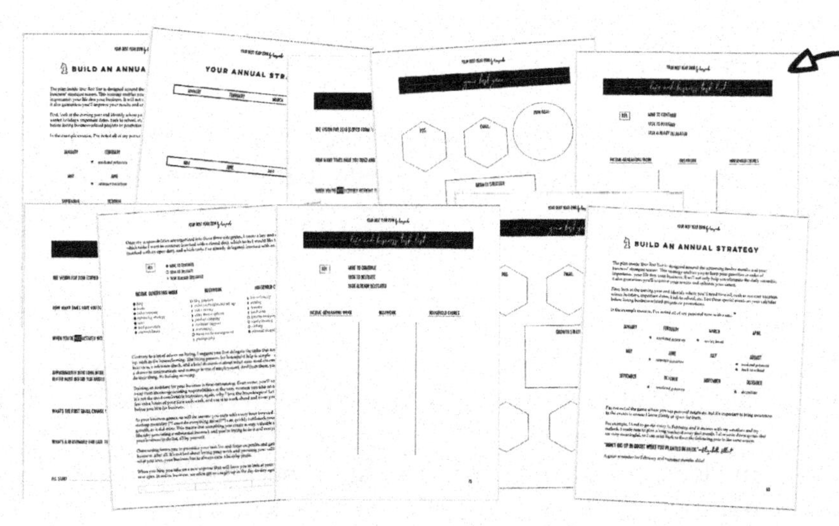

Next, you'll create a clear vision of the goals you plan to reach, to include all of the motivating reasons you want to achieve it.

Here, you'll create a strategy that will empower your annual goals. This section will ensure your success.

Finally, you'll create an airtight schedule for when you'll work and what you'll focus on.

Your monthly action plan will help define who you need to become in order to create and attract the success you crave.

SURVIVAL OF THE FITTEST

I have a shocking story to share with you. It's a tale of quitters who seemingly had it all (great website, self-confidence, professional showmanship, etc.), but they simply couldn't hang.

A few years ago, I created a list on Twitter of local online businesses. I checked back a few months ago—the majority (at least 95%, if not more) gave up on their entrepreneurial pursuits. Designers switched to other career fields, writers took 9-5 editing jobs, bloggers left the building, and shop owners vacated the premises.

Some of these quitters had very specific dreams, and at one time, they took their pursuit of those dreams very seriously. I don't give admiration freely, and I genuinely admired these bloggers and business owners for the work that they did. Years ago, I was intimidated to contact them. I reached out to collaborate or connect—most ignored me.

They threw in the towel after nine months or two years or too few visitors. Each one of them created a unique excuse, convinced themselves they didn't want that dream *anyway,* and high-tailed it back to an easier path toward a cozy (albeit average) comfort zone.

I get it. I've almost convinced myself the same several times during my career.

And it's not just entrepreneurs. By January 15, 95% of people will have given up on their freshly set New Year's resolutions. If that's how impatient our craving for instant gratification is, no wonder people quit their businesses!

Ever since I discovered they had all quit, I've been fascinated by what makes some people persist despite the odds. At the time, I had a truly scary thought: What if I had quit too? Because the struggle is real. I plugged away at my own business for over four years wondering what I was doing wrong and why I couldn't shatter the glass income ceiling over my head.

What if I had tucked my tail between my legs, left Marketing Creativity™ because "it'll never work," and started all over in a more traditional career? What if I'd never created the Luminaries Club™ (my private membership program), written *Your Best Year*, or instructed on CreativeLive? What if I hadn't pushed through the frustration to tap into my full potential? How much of *myself* would I have missed out on?

Short-changing my vision of success is a much scarier alternative to the risks I've taken. If there's a thing you can't *not* build, a talent you *must* express, or a better life you know you were *meant* to live, I believe it is your duty to pursue it with everything you have.

I've heard a lot of noise lately about not setting goals—big mistake. HUGE! I spend weeks in review and reflection every year because, you not only need goals, you need to set your mind right in order to barrel-roll through them.

This year I knew that, in order to help you reach your full potential, I'd have to show you why people bail on themselves. What makes people quit when they seemingly have everything going for them? It is so clear to the rest of us, from the outside in, that they're only steps away from striking the gold for which they'd been prospecting.

As for the Twitter list, it wasn't that they didn't have a great product. It wasn't that they didn't know how to run a business. It certainly wasn't a matter of content, photography, or branding.

When any of us say, "I can't do this for one more day," it's not literal (though it does feel true at the time). That statement is made out of frustration and burn-out, lack of motivation or perspective, absence of gain or results, or any combination of the above.

The Twitter quitters failed to survive and endure. You and I both know it's hard, but until this year, I didn't even realize how many forces and instincts were fighting against us.

The Forces Against You

The human brain is a two-million-year-old organ that's been programmed to sustain and preserve your life force. Because its main function is to ensure your survival, it is human nature to put more value on what you might *lose* and less value on what you stand to *gain*.

The brain is also a miraculous super computer between your ears. When used creatively, we're not even sure how to access its full potential! Nobody's even figured that out yet; we just hope Elon Musk will show the rest of us how to use a little more of its imaginative powers.

Though you have unlimited access to new ideas and opportunities, your brain's default response to risk is to flee from danger and run to safety. At its very core, the brain *loves* a comfort zone like no other, and almost everything you do to create positive change or grow, in any aspect of life, involves some risk.

As you read this, there are risks in business that are begging you to take a chance. On the other side of those risks is either experience gained or your desires achieved. For me, there have been no mistakes in business; I walk away a winner from every risk taken, even when I lose.

In *Your Best Year 2018,* you'll come to understand how YOU are standing in the way of achieving your wildest dreams. You'll realize that you probably make more decisions out of fear than you do out of desire. You will notice how you often stop yourself *before you even begin.* You'll identify where you've been trying to reach extraordinary goals with very ordinary actions, hence your results remain very ordinary.

"THERE ARE RISKS AND COSTS TO ACTION. BUT THEY ARE FAR LESS THAN THE LONG RANGE RISKS OF COMFORTABLE INACTION."—John F. Kennedy

When you set out to create the best year of your life, you will face uncertainty and risk. Both are very uncomfortable, which is why 95% of people avoid them at all costs. Rather than avoid risk, you must learn how to embrace it at every pass. You can rise above the brain's instinctive signals of fear and panic to break the default routine that is "keeping you safe" (and stuck).

When people are in panic mode, they have no idea what they're doing or WHY, so they rely on outworn patterns and old routines. They do more of what's *not* working.

Every summer, without fail, I start worrying about the state of my business. It doesn't matter if I landed a book deal and earned six-figures in May, and it doesn't matter that things always pick back up in the fall. Every June, traffic slows, engagement dries up, and I start worrying. By July, the worry has surfaced into a thinly-veiled panic. In August, I'm a tornado of stress, searching the internet for places to submit my resume.

Come September, I'm happy as a peach and back to my routine.

The other things that happen every summer? I take more time off. I set less deadlines. I take less actions. I spend my working hours on things that don't generate profit (namely, social media and "research" on Pinterest). My bank account dwindles. I forget my goals. I lose the vision. I worry, then panic, until I become utterly lost in the jungle.

My friends, that behavior results in sure failure, not survival. And I know you can relate because it happens to us all. The real question here is: What changes in September? Well, there's a deadline on the horizon, so I have to stop "researching" the next project, open the file, and get to work. I feel instantly empowered again after one solid day of forward progress.

"NOTHING HAPPENS UNTIL SOMETHING MOVES."—Albert Einstein

Your success means the difference between your auto-responder reaction (when you find yourself emotional and panicked about the current state of affairs) versus taking action and methodically plugging away toward long-term gain.

It is always a mistake to think you can limit yourself and expand at the same time.

Last year, I made the decision to change. This part is so simple that it's both scary and heartbreaking because we limit ourselves every day. I moved toward change. I made decisions as though I were already running a six-figure business. I had to act like that successful business owner before I could become her. This year, I'm going to call on you to do the same.

It's Time to Hurdle Your Obstacles

How do you get from where you are to where you want to be? You physically move toward it; you take the actions necessary to get you there. If you wanted to travel from Pittsburgh to New

York, you can't sit down on a park bench in Pittsburgh and wonder why you're not getting to New York.

It seems too simple to be true, but few people actively take action toward their goals. Most people are sitting on a park bench in Pittsburgh complaining about how their dreams aren't showing up for them. Can New York show up in Pittsburgh? No!

I do four specific things to bring my vision of success to life every year. I make …

- my goals resolute,
- my strategies specific,
- my system efficient, and
- my action plan productive.

Before I established this structure, I wasn't hitting my goals. I was treading water—doing a lot of work and getting nowhere for it. Since incorporating this plan, my business has taken flight.

In this book, I'm going to show you how to create the same results. This year's *Your Best Year* is a refresher on the fundamentals. You'll review what is and isn't working, identify what needs to change, challenge your limitations, and figure out what to focus on. Then, you'll take calculated risks that will help you soar to the next level.

Before We Begin

I need to know where your head is at. Lately, I've been fixated on the mindset gap between a starving artist and a hungry entrepreneur. Let's compare.

The starving artist's mentality is one of sacrifice and suffering. They are more likely starved mentally and spiritually rather than physically, unable to feed an insatiable craving for validation. They exist in a state of helpless desperation, too rejection-weary to persist. Starving artists convince themselves that success means selling out, but this is simply a justification used to excuse their lack of business-building efforts.

—OR—

The hungry entrepreneur's mentality is one of opportunity and determination. This is a person on the hunt for their next win. Starved for nothing, they seek a personal vision of success and take complete responsibility for its realization. Hungry entrepreneurs are on the build, primed for their next chance to create the results they desire.

See the difference?

Now, let me give you the choice. Which personality above do you want to buy from? The hungry entrepreneur, of course! You aren't going to shop a weary excuse of an offer. You're not attracted to needy desperation. You don't want to give your money with an added tip of reassurance and validation. Nobody chooses to be drained by emotional vampires!

More importantly, which personality are you going to choose to be?

The starving artist mentality is the path of least resistance. It's easy to make excuses and justifications for why you're not achieving your desired results. Anyone can want and not change. Anyone can name their weakness and excuse it as incompetence. Most people do!

I don't care who you are, human beings are attracted to leaders and winners. They're drawn to true performers who are willing to take the stage. In order for people to receive your business with warmth and excitement, you must believe in its success and your abilities long before you ask for a sale.

You are 100% responsible. I used to say you're half of every relationship you're involved in (whether it's good or bad). I've since been schooled. Darren Hardy showed me the way when he quoted this life-changing advice from a seminar he attended at eighteen:

> "What percentage of shared responsibility do you have in making a relationship work? 100/0. You have to be willing to give 100 percent with zero expectation of receiving anything in return. Only when you're willing to take 100 percent responsibility for making the relationship work will it work. Otherwise, a relationship left to chance will always be vulnerable to disaster."

Your business profits say a lot about your level of responsibility to it. It speaks to how committed you are, the risks you're willing to take, the time and money you're willing to invest, and the success you believe you deserve.

"EVEN AFTER ALL THIS TIME, THE SUN NEVER SAYS TO THE EARTH, 'YOU OWE ME.' LOOK WHAT HAPPENS WITH A LOVE LIKE THAT. IT LIGHTS THE WHOLE SKY."—Hafiz

If you're ready to change your current trajectory and launch toward your own next level success, you too must ask yourself what the next level version of you would DO. Then, you must take those actions now.

What to Focus on

Too often you get caught up in doing for doing's sake in online business. You might make products even though your current inventory's not moving (making for making's sake), post status updates online even though what you're saying isn't connecting (marketing for marketing's sake), email because you know you're supposed to (emailing for emailing's sake), and research everything you can find online to try to make what isn't working *work already* (training for training's sake).

You probably find yourself getting swept away by a lot of business-building ideas that don't even make sense, such as "Open another storefront" (when you already have one storefront that's not selling), or "Grow my account on Twitter" (when none of your customers/clients even use that platform), or "Start Periscoping" (because it's the latest random advice floating around *all of the other* social platforms that day).

None of it matters. It's all doing for doing's sake. You don't need two storefronts anymore than I need two blogs! It will only create more things that don't matter to fuss over. It's scrambling, and you're better than that! Your work deserves more attention, your time is extremely valuable, and your business is meant to give back!

To grow a successful online business you need a website that attracts and converts, a marketing strategy that wins, and a plan to optimize numbers one and two.

Therefore, don't open more storefronts if the original site isn't working. Instead, spend your time and energy improving your existing storefront! Don't open new social media accounts if you're not connecting with the profiles you already have. Instead, study the platform with the most potential to grow your following through the roof!

If you're in online business, you've likely heard of the Pareto principle (aka the 80/20 rule) which states that (from Wikipedia), "For many events, roughly 80% of the effects come from 20% of the causes." For example—and those of you who have an email list will know this to be true—80% of your revenue comes from 20% of your customers.

The reason this rule is examined in the online world is because it's a hack for doing more of what matters to your bottom line. If 20% of your working hours produce 80% of your results, then that means that the other 80% of the time you spend produces only 20% of your desired results. How would your results improve if you focused all of your attention on the 20% of work that adds to 80% of your bottom line? That's what we're going to explore in this section.

Ask yourself the following questions to find out which 20% of your applied efforts are producing 80% of your desired results:

- What was your best business payday of all time?
- Where do you invest energy without return?

Your working hours should always result in one of two things:

1. Growth (*Will it attract email subscribers and traffic?*), and/or
2. Profit (*Will it make money for my business?*)

If your hours don't result in either of those things (meaning, you're fussing, checking, or otherwise doing for doing's sake), it's not helping your business' bottom line. When you write a list of tasks you need to do for your business, always ask—**to what end?**

- To what end are you building another website?
- To what end are you blogging?
- To what end are you creating a new social media account?
- To what end are you emailing?

Attach one of your desired outcomes to every action you take. If you can't attach an end goal, you shouldn't be doing it.

Make the Decision

Anytime you face risk or diversity, the brain (that super computer organ with two-million-year-old instincts) kicks on its warning system. It presses the panic button and releases a dose of cortisol—a stress hormone. The brain's autoresponder reaction magnifies the danger of the risk so you will crawl back into your comfort zone, safe and sound.

As a result, you pump the brakes on your business endeavors.

Time and time again, something ruffles your feathers, and you doubt your abilities. You second-guess your direction. You reduce your goals. I don't say this just in case, it's a given. Fear will creep in on you, and in response, you'll slow your barrel roll to a stop and question everything.

This is why improved decision-making contributes to overall mental toughness. You have to stop him-hawing on trivial decisions (*Should I buy that book? Should I upgrade my equipment? Should I invest in this business training? Do I really need new branding?*), and make the easy choices your business requires of you, right now.

Do you want your brain pumping cortisol over a $10 book? Of course not! Don't waste precious energy on insignificant risks. It will significantly reduce your chance of survival.

In order to have a breakthrough year, you will need to take giant leaps and big risks. It will require brutal courage and savage intention. When it comes time to do the things that truly scare you, you can't *hope* you'll hit your target as you incessantly pump the brakes. Instead, bounce on the devil and put the pedal to the floor. You have to smash through that goal.

Decisions will be your rescue or your doom based on whether you make them out of fear or desire. Avoiding them (especially the ones involving life- or business-improvements) typically compounds the problem leading to even more difficult choices. Moreover, indecisive people become a victim of circumstance.

It is the opposite of taking 100% responsibility for your success.

I avoid indecisiveness like it's the plague. I give my full attention to the decisions at hand, so I can put them to rest as quickly as possible. If I find myself procrastinating on an issue or it requires more than I have on hand to draw a conclusion, I assign a deadline (e.g., Friday at noon) for when it must be decided.

Because of this approach, I never complain about my situation in life or business. I plow through decisions to take the lead.

Trust the Business to Provide

Of all things, pure and utter faith in your pursuits is the hardest thing to fabricate in entrepreneurship. In order to make big things happen, you have to trust your business to provide and barrel-roll through your goals.

Two of the toughest questions I answer every year are:

- Do you trust your business to provide?
- Do you trust yourself to follow through on what's required?

Many of us are so afraid of expenses—we look at upgrades as a direct loss. It's only during the decision-making process that it feels that way; as soon as you make the decision, you instantly feel richer and do better. This is true for both personal and professional aspects, in fact, they often intertwine.

For example, I chased the same financial issue in my mind for years. My eldest daughter was self-conscious about her smile; the older she got, the more crooked her front teeth became. I had a good idea of how much braces cost, but there were always bills or other financial priorities in the way.

Around the time I was upgrading my business (and after two years of fussing over the cost of orthodontic care), I booked an appointment. I wasn't sure how I was going to pay for the braces, but I took my daughter in for a consultation anyway.

At the consultation, I immediately agreed to the cost and terms of service. I decided that I was done chasing this problem; I was just going to solve it. My daughter exploded into happy tears as I filled out the final paperwork.

And then, the most magical thing happened. I made enough to cover the entire bill within two weeks of signing the contract. She hadn't even started treatment, yet I had paid her account in full. The moral of the story—I finally trusted my business to provide, and so it did.

There's a hidden floodgate of abundance behind obstacles such as these, but first you need to allow your business to provide!

Survivors behave as though they're going to survive, *no matter what*. They see beyond the circumstances, they trust the process and themselves. They recognize panic as a temporary side effect to the situation rather than an emotion to adopt. They find inner strength and certainty in highly uncertain conditions, and they focus on the only things they have control over: their actions, reactions, and ideas.

I want you to do the same. You will face fear. There will be uncertainty. Situations will regularly challenge you. Reactionary emotions are normal, but you have total control over what you *do* next. Will you succumb to the panic rising up within you and let it spread into a mass of stress and anxiety?

—OR—

Will you trust the business to provide and make decisions that ensure your survival?

Here are the exact steps I took before the biggest profit breakthrough of my life, and it's no coincidence that I made all of these changes **90 days** before the money arrived (more on this in the final chapter of the book):

1. I trusted my business to provide.
2. I trusted my ability to earn good money.
3. I made a personal finance decision that forced me to *prove* it.
4. I showed up and did the work, giving more than I ever had before.

Just imagine—is there even a limit to what you could create if you gave your absolute best for thirty days in a row, acting as though it were impossible to fail?

Do you know how rare that is—that someone gives their best for thirty days straight? Let's be honest, most people don't give thirty best days a *year*! Do you realize how easy it would be to stand out in the crowd with that kind of work ethic?

It might not be possible to give 100% day in and day out, but through my system this year, I'm going to ask you to regularly give *more*—I know you have it in you. I want you to become an endurance entrepreneur.

What would happen if, this year, you took all the emotion, stress, and fervor that high achievers have in common out of the equation? What if instead you follow the techniques in this book, repeat simply daily disciplines toward the goals that matter every day, no matter what?

ARE YOU READY FOR THE NEXT LEVEL?

trust-building exercise

WHAT DECISION HAVE YOU BEEN HIM-HAWING ABOUT, CHASING ON AND ON FOR ABSOLUTELY NO REASON?

Blogging & writing a newsletter
Building up a newsletter base.

WHAT EMBARRASSES YOU THE MOST ABOUT YOUR CURRENT OPERATION?

- That I haven't gotten off the 1st fl.
- That I haven't committed to the above
Social media but I'm not that into it

WHAT ARE YOU HOLDING YOURSELF BACK FROM UPGRADING IN YOUR BUSINESS?

My website but I just took that action this week.
Social media & Instagram -

IN WHAT AREAS ARE YOU FAILING TO TRUST YOUR BUSINESS TO PROVIDE?

Mostly in me to sell & close
I am worth the money

WHAT'S THE FIRST STEP, CALL, OR CONSULTATION YOU CAN MAKE TOWARD YOUR UPGRADE?

call Lauree & tell her that I'm holding off for right now.

ENDURANCE ENTREPRENEUR

How Bad Do You Want it? Mastering the Psychology of Mind Over Muscle by Matt Fitzgerald is a book about endurance athletes that has forever changed the way I do business. It taught me more about entrepreneurship in 265 pages than I'd learned after tens of thousands of dollars worth of training and seven years of experience. It's *that* relevant to what we do, and I highly recommend you go get a copy right now.

I'll share quotes from *How Bad Do You Want It?* throughout this book, and where you see the word [entrepreneur] inside brackets, I've simply replaced "athlete" with "entrepreneur;" that's how strong the same statements apply. For example, "The more discomfort an [entrepreneur] expects, the more she can tolerate, and the more she can tolerate, the better she can perform."

Business is a game involving stress, resistance, uncertainty, and discomfort. Success is as much about coping with these unsettling factors as it is about achieving goals. Fitzgerald teaches two very important lessons for our purposes: coping techniques and perception of effort.

Effective **coping methods** cultivate mental fitness. You need a survivor's mindset to battle the resistance, uncertainty, and discomfort you face in business. Those uncomfortable emotions are well-known hazards; the reason 90% of entrepreneurs won't survive.

Coping methods are a set of behaviors, emotions, and thought patterns that are prepared ahead to help you respond to the challenges you are guaranteed to face on your path to greatness.

Coping methods can be effective or ineffective, and we'll be studying the effective ones here. Some examples of ineffective coping methods are: hoping things won't be hard (and bailing because nothing's easy), procrastination and avoidance (to escape reality and the work at hand), productivity tension (the restlessness created when you're not doing what you know needs done), and underperforming (with the pretense that you're giving it your all).

Perception of effort is how hard you *feel* like you're working. As mentioned in the previous chapter, when someone says, "I can't do this for one more day," it's not literal. The individual is sharing their sense of how hard they feel like they're working under difficult circumstances.

There's probably been a time in your life when you've experienced this in athletics. You run so hard that your perception of effort feels maxed out. When you stop running (and cease applying the effort you perceived as very hard), you feel immediate relief. It's not like you "can't go on." In fact, afterwards you go right back to your day.

"PERCEPTION OF EFFORT IS THE FEELING OF ACTIVITY IN THE BRAIN THAT STIMULATES WORK; IT IS NOT THE FEELING OF WORK ITSELF."—Matt Fitzgerald

Nothing can convince your mind that it's only a feeling during the exertion, though. When you perceive yourself as gassed out, Fitzgerald says, "resistance exists nowhere in particular yet also everywhere." It *feels* impossible to go on.

Perception of effort effects how you perform at challenges (and whether or not you think you can overcome them). It contributes to fear and stress (the harder you feel like you're working, the more stressed or panicked you'll be). It increases self-doubt, second-guessing, errors, and mistakes (when the going gets tough).

Perception of effort is the primary source of discomfort. It's also the same force that compels you to dig deep and make that final push toward the finish line.

And what I love about perception of effort is that it can be hacked. In fitness, the more you workout, the easier the workout becomes. Why? Because the fitter you get, the easier the workout *feels*. The effort remains the same (same routine, same exertion, same time) while your *perception* of effort greatly decreases. The easier it feels, the more you can tolerate, the better you perform.

Now, here's how all of this applies to business. We cannot change the fact that there will be resistance, uncertainty, and discomfort going forward. We can, however, employ effective coping methods that will favorably change perception of effort toward these matters.

There are countless coping methods to explore in *How Bad Do You Want It?*, but I've narrowed them down to my favorite five for online businesses.

#1 Find the Flow

Flow is what happens when you dive into the work and completely lose sight of everything else. It's a wavelength of creation that's free of all distractions or emotional static. It's a clear channel of production, in which you're tuned in and everything outside of the task is turned off.

Flow is a beautiful state of laser-focused attention that results in significant progress or improvement of skill.

The best way to fabricate flow in online business is to time-block your working hours, using a method similar to the Pomodoro Technique (25 minutes of focused work separated by short breaks, developed by Francesco Cirillo). I call mine "powerblocks," and I set a timer for anywhere from 50-90 minutes, depending on the task.

I lengthened my powerblocks (up from 25 minutes) because I found that it took me 10-15 minutes to tune everything out and achieve the flow state, only to be interrupted 10 minutes later when the traditional Pomodoro timer went off. I start at 25-minute intervals and increase them over time until I figure out what works best for any given project.

By definition, there can be no distractions during the flow state. The point is to forget yourself, and the world around you, and attend to the task at hand.

"ENDURANCE ATHLETES DESCRIBE THE FLOW STATE AS ONE IN WHICH THEY SEEM TO BECOME THE THING THEY ARE DOING."—Matt Fitzgerald

It's not that you think more clearly in flow; it is as though you're not thinking at all. Instead, you *become* a clear channel of pure production. It is undiluted action at its finest. It's empowerment in the form of progress, and eventually completion.

This state cannot be achieved if your phone's going off every 10 minutes because you're simultaneously texting with a friend while you work. This dedicated stream of production does not run in the background while you check Facebook. It can only occur when you are 100% present for it.

I alluded to this earlier, with the story of my routine annual summer panic. As I said, I take more time off during summer break. I set less deadlines. I encourage my children to interrupt me; I actively avoid flow so I can be present with them. Therefore, I take less action, which leads to overthinking and underachieving. The missing ingredient to my summers is flow—scheduled, distraction-free progress that results in my becoming a clear channel of production.

This coping method is the difference between getting spun up *thinking* about the work and actually doing it.

#2 Refine the Pace

Around the time I started in online business (almost 10 years ago), I took up running as an outlet to help with all of the pent up energy, nerves, and excitement that come with the job. Within a year, I increased my speed and endurance so that I could run several miles, at pace.

"FROM THAT DAY ON, IF I WAS GOING SOMEWHERE, I WAS RUNNING."—Forrest Gump

I fell in love with the movement, like freedom on the wings, and I was so proud of how fast I'd become on my feet. When I spotted another fast runner on the road, the competitive nature in me would kick in, and I would surge forward to take the lead and show off my speed. I was so excited to have someone to race that my heart would start pounding, my breath would shallow, I'd lose speed, and start sucking air.

That's called choking, and it's the exact opposite of flow.

From *How Bad Do You Want It?*, "If choking is a condition of heightened self-consciousness that intensifies perceived effort and hampers endurance performance, then its opposite would be [flow] a mental state in which self-consciousness disappears, reducing perceived effort and boosting performance."

In other words, rather than finding the flow and enjoying the run, my heightened awareness of racing caused me to choke. The same thing happens in business.

How many times have you leapt into action, gung-ho on a new idea, only to completely abandon it days later? Most people attempt to change in brief fits and spurts of motivation. They enter the race at the fastest speeds, in a state of extreme self-consciousness, impede the flow, and ultimately hinder their desired results.

Instead (and like an endurance athlete), you need to find the most aggressive pace that can be sustained over time. This year, I want you to refine your pace by creating a schedule that allows you to methodically chip away at your workload rather than maniacally chase deadlines and demand. I'll show you how to create a schedule with margin, and it will ensure you keep the flow in your routine from one day to the next, without choking.

You also need a rhythm of production and completion. By employing this coping method, you will train yourself to complete one project before starting another (because you do it way more often than you realize!).

#3 Compete to Add Fuel

I won't lie; I have played the comparison game plenty of times throughout my career. We've all compared ourselves to others, to see how we stack up. Worse yet, we all keep talking about the comparison game and how it plagues us in online business, but what we should be asking is, why do we all feel so compelled to compare in the first place?

The fact of the matter is, we are struggling collectively, but for reasons unknown, we each insist on going about it alone. Instead of becoming a growing industry, we stubbornly maintain our individual proprietorship. Instead of creating systems for coping, each of us shares the "perfect face" of our singular achievements. We lack connection, we crave teamwork.

We embark on the comparison game for reasons innocent enough. At the heart of the search, we're seeking camaraderie, someone to relate to our plight. However, when we fail to connect (because we all hide our shadow sides), it compounds the very struggle we set out to resolve.

Here's how the game looks on me. When I'm not getting anything done, I look around at what everyone else is doing, which in turn conjures up a wide variety of emotions: resentment, superiority, jealousy, envy, and contempt. I dwell there for a bit. It's entirely unproductive. It results in shame. It triggers panic. It's an unhealthy cycle (and *everybody* does it sometimes).

On the other hand, when I'm fighting the good fight and working diligently toward my goals, a little healthy competition gives me LIFE. It's fuel. In *How Bad Do You Want It?*, the comparison game was considered locker room fodder. For the first time ever, I realized this could be a good and healthy thing! How can you turn the colossal waste of time that is the comparison game into a lesson of empowerment?

The next time you find yourself caught up in the comparison game, ask yourself:

- What bothers me about this? Why am I feeling resentful or envious of their situation?
- What do they have that I want?
- Why do I feel contempt? What do I see them gaining that I think I deserve?
- What do I find bothersome or offensive about their approach or presence online?
- What do I sense they're doing better than me? What am I *not* doing that they're doing well?
- If the feeling is mutual add: What bothers them about me?

Therein lie your answers: What bothers you about your competitor are your current weak points in business. Maybe they have an extra dose of confidence, and you're still waiting for recognition and approval from external forces. Maybe they present themselves as important or qualified, and you haven't perfected the art of self-promotion yet. Maybe they seem to be releasing one best-seller after another, and you feel far from completion on *anything*.

Whatever it is, it's a chance to strengthen your game. And if the feeling is mutual, you have all the more locker room fodder fuel! What bothers them about you is an area you can continue to enhance, and maybe even show off a bit more. Maybe it's your industry knowledge and high-quality goods. Maybe it's your expertise or promising sales projection. In any case, show it off!

Constant improvement leads to constant expansion, and if some healthy competition motivates you, then channel it accordingly. See? Empowerment!

If you have a competitive nature, enjoy playing the game. It is okay to win. It's okay to be defeated. Put a competitor in your sights right now and start chasing them down! It's a great coping method for endurance, and it offers a genuine opportunity to improve.

#4 Brace Yourself

If you aim to change and evolve this year—if you're in it to win it and ready to make it happen, which I assume you are—then you also have to prepare yourself for discomfort. It's a given, and if you're not prepared for it, things will feel impossible and that feeling will be your undoing.

"HARD CHOICES, EASY LIFE. EASY CHOICES, HARD LIFE."—Jerzy Gregorek

Tony Robbins says, "Success leaves clues," and I've spent the year amongst successful *giants:* buried in between the pages of their books, listening to their Ted Talks, attending their conferences, and taking their training programs. I've studied Tony, Grant Cardone, Mel Robbins, Jeb Blount, Dr. Christiane Northrup, Gary Keller, Tim Ferris, Ramit Sethi, Matt Fitzgerald, Darren Hardy, and many more.

The one thing that each of them states in plain English, the common thread among them all, was this: you must forego the confines of your comfort zone in order to make great things happen. You have to think outside of it, push past it, and aim to shatter it time and time again.

If you haven't yet achieved the success you crave, comfort is the culprit. There is too much comfort somewhere in your life, whether it be in your daily routine, your style of marketing, the content or product you create, or how much of yourself you're willing to reveal.

Anytime you feel restless and dissatisfied, you can blame comfort. It's the soft bed that's much easier than a hard, AM workout. It's the social media time that's much easier than project completion. If you're dissatisfied today, look at all the comfortable choices you made yesterday.

When you find yourself coming up against tough decisions, challenges, obstacles, or demands, you must remember—it's not impossible, it's only hard (and that's okay, you'll survive).

"IF IT IS ENDURABLE, THEN ENDURE IT. STOP COMPLAINING."—Marcus Aurelius

Successful people are willing to do what most people won't. It's that old adage about going the extra mile, and you better get your start now. The more people that catch on, the easier it will be to get success, and the harder it will be for any one of us to stand out!

#5 Want it More

In response to his own question—How bad do you want it?—Fitzgerald says your answer always has to be, "More."

How much can you accomplish this year? If you went balls to the wall, agreed to some discomfort, really—how much do you think you could get done? It's not about money or sales or numbers, even though you'll definitely see an increase if you play along. Instead, it is about completion, follow-through, and endurance. That's a beautiful thing because those attributes are well within your control.

WHAT IF, THIS YEAR, YOU DIDN'T HOLD BACK?

What if you pushed passed all of your limits to see how far you might go? What if you didn't let a slow period slow you down? Do you see the unlimited potential in that idea? Make the commitment right now. I'm not going to run you into the ground on this commitment. I don't mean all work and no joy. I do not intend to let you crash and burn out.

What I do need you to do, is promise that you won't pump the brakes because of low motivation. Low motivation is an excuse. We all have those days. I need you to be tougher than that. When the goal suddenly feels too hard to reach, I need you to promise you will fight harder for it rather than reduce it. You have it in you, let's see you do it.

STATE OF THE UNION

State of the Union speeches are my new thing. I like to kickoff my training programs by accurately describing the current conditions the industry is facing, and then follow up with a plan on how to tackle the most pressing issues.

You will use this section to do the same thing, but first you'll need to decide what you are willing to change once and for all.

Every year on my blog, I lead a series titled "A New Year for a New You: 7 Days of Review" which includes prompts similar to the ones you are about to fill out. During the series, I offer readers a new list of review questions each day. I then blog my answers from the previous day before issuing the next set of prompts.

When I write that series, I always go back on previous years to collect questions and ideas for the current year. A few years in, my "New Year for a New You" reflections were responsible for a life-changing wake-up call.

Most people don't have the advantage of reviewing their previous goals and challenges each year, but I have a five-year public record of mine. As I reviewed past series to copy questions (Where is time being wasted? What are your biggest challenges? What were your worst setbacks?), I realized I might as well be copying all the answers, too!

What I planned to discuss in 2014 were the same problems I'd written in 2013. Looking back a year further, I found the same challenges, setbacks, and bad habits again! I couldn't believe my eyes. I was keeping my problems year after year.

As I read back over three years' worth of the same relationship problems, financial setbacks, weight issues, and bad habits, I got emotional. That moment still makes me tear up today. It broke my heart that I wasn't making positive changes for myself, that I was unknowingly so reluctant to make the choices that would create a better life.

I urge you to ask yourself: Are you better off now than you were a year ago in all five pillars of life: emotional, spiritual, relational, financial, and mental?

I've learned that we get very comfortable with our obstacles, for one reason or another:

- We like the nurturing it brings from the outside world.
- We're addicted to the dramatics an unsolved problem adds to our life.
- (Most likely) We feel overwhelmed, uncertain, and too scared to take the first step in the right direction.

Is there something in your life—your weight, your health, your career, your income, your relationships—that you've been struggling with for far too long?

People keep their problems because change is hard. Before you reap the rewards, you have to crawl through a slew of challenging obstacles and emotions. I won't sugarcoat this for you; I want you to be prepared.

Prepare to face uncertainty and stare down your biggest fears. Prepare to do your best work without guaranteed results or fanfare. Prepare to face negativity, frustration, and criticism. Prepare to confuse and baffle; most people will have long since given up while you continue to persist.

The extreme minority insist on solving their problems rather than adapting to them. Five percent of people in this world …

- Achieve extreme wealth
- Operate successful businesses
- Take their career to the highest level
- Create exceptional health and fitness habits
- Nurture clean and loving relationships
- Strengthen their spiritual and mental weaknesses

If any of these things were easy to achieve, everyone would have them. Prepare yourself now; your goals are out there, like a destination on a map, awaiting your arrival.

Sweet Disgust

If you look back on the changes you've previously made in your life, you will probably find they all have something in common: a turning point in which you felt a sense of angry resolve. Right before a giant breakthrough, most people decide they can't afford *not to change*.

People don't get motivated—they get mad. From *How Bad Do You Want It?*

> "Robert Wicks, a psychologist and author of the book *Bounce: Living the Resilient Life*, has referred to this type of angry resolve as 'sweet disgust.' The phrase aptly conveys the idea that there is an element of healthy wrath in the fed-up mind state that fuels positive change. Sweet disgust is really the opposite of defeat. It is a determination to fight back, something that is hard to do effectively without anger. All else being equal, the angrier party in a fight wins."

As you work through the following review, pay as much attention, if not more, to what's *not* working as you do what *is* working..

What situations, unresolved issues, and frustrating circumstances are you ready to get mad at?

what is working?

WHAT ARE YOUR FAVORITE MEMORIES OF 2017?

Spending time w/J - the beach - Ellie & Rachel - Gerstens - Ira
Doing my step work -
wking w/ Rochelle - Wild Quest.
Any good coaching sessions / WW meeting. Xmas w/ Lisa & Maggie - Making BBQ Sauce
Going to museums theatre -
Getting my nails done

WHAT WAS TIME VERY WELL SPENT?

- 12 step work - meetings
- Creating GTK
- Wild Quest
- Anytime the TV isn't turned on.
- Reading
- Always being w family & friends.
- Spending time on SMP/GTK

WHAT DID YOU ACCOMPLISH OR COMPLETE?

- I finished my UA steps
- I started being focused w/ wk -
- Losing weight
- keeping the apt cleaner
- Bullet Journaling

WHAT WAS MONEY VERY WELL SPENT?

- Wking w/ Rochelle -
- Wild Quest -
- Jolene
- Bullet Journals
- skin care makeup nails - brows
- theatre

DID YOU MAKE ANY PROGRESS ON BIG LIFE GOALS IN 2017?

Yes - I'm launching GTK -
my health has improved -
Wking on my Alanon issues
keeping my ~~[illegible]~~'s

example answers

WHAT ARE YOUR FAVORITE MEMORIES OF 2017?

- *First year in our new home*
- *Exploring our new neighborhood*
- *Weekend getaway to Charleston, SC*
- *20th wedding anniversary*
- *Our first movie at the Alamo—Guardians II*
- *Playing at Top Golf*
- *Filming live with Luminaries*
- *Booking training, venues, and travel for business without fear*

WHAT WAS TIME VERY WELL SPENT?

- *All work toward project completion was time extremely well spent*
- *Downtime with my family—indulging in simple pleasures was a great reward*
- *Studying business, strengthening weaknesses*
- *Reading romance novels and fiction*
- *Weekly review and planning*
- *Traveling with my family*
- *Taking an entire day to go wardrobe shopping for myself, by myself*

WHAT DID YOU ACCOMPLISH OR COMPLETE?

- *Lost ten pounds*
- *Got children situated and thriving in a new school district*
- *Hired first FT employee for business*
- *Finished and cleared tax mess*
- *Launched new web design*
- *Launched Marketing Playbook*
- *Grand re-opening of the Luminaries Club™*
- *Trademarked my business names*
- *Hosted a free three-part training series*
- *Launched Your Best Year 2018*
- *Hosted my own workshop (offline)*

WHAT WAS MONEY VERY WELL SPENT?

- *Housecleaning!*
- *My assistant, Jennie and support staff*
- *Taxes paid in full—to be free and clear*
- *New wardrobe that was thoughtfully planned for my lifestyle*
- *Everything professional: Design, development, and photography*
- *Home office remodel*
- *Professional video equipment*
- *Accounting and bookkeeping services*

DID YOU MAKE ANY PROGRESS ON BIG LIFE GOALS IN 2017?

My goal for 2017 was to create more assets and security, in both life and business. I spent more time getting things done than I did making memories. My professional task list has been full and productive.

The idea was to front-load a number of projects, and use the year to finish my portfolio of signature offerings, so that I can spend more time leveraging those assets. If my plan works, it will free more time for enjoying my life. We'll see if my upfront investment pays off, but I completed these projects to make significant progress on big life goals this year.

what is working?

WHAT FELT SUCCESSFUL ABOUT 2017?

- I saved money to spend on Wild Quest & my business
- I lost weight
- I'm finding my voice
-

WHAT DID YOU LEARN ABOUT YOURSELF?

- I'm happier when I watch less TV
- I can grow regardless of J
- I am good at what I do
- I am teachable.

DID YOU OVERCOME ANY OBSTACLES?

Yes - I had a nervous break down & am rebuilding & recreating myself.
Taking action steps w/ SMP - GTK.
Finding new friends.

WHO NURTURED AND SUPPORTED YOU?

- Linda & Jim flexible
- Noemi - believes in me openheart
- Joele helps me online stuff - & picking up doing the dishes
- Rochelle - guidance
- UPP group feedback
- UA group - positive feedback

WHO DID YOU ENJOY NURTURING AND SUPPORTING?

example answers

WHAT FELT SUCCESSFUL ABOUT 2017?

- *Re-strategizing my approach. I learn a lot from what works and what doesn't, and I love tearing everything down to build it back up again the right way. I've done this both in business and for our personal finances.*
- *Getting things done. I don't love how much I worked this year, or how intense the schedule was, but I crossed things off my to-do list that had been nagging me for years.*
- *My marriage. It's been twenty years of growing up together, and we still find new ways to love and support each other every day.*

DID YOU OVERCOME ANY OBSTACLES?

The entire year felt like an obstacle of growth and change, and I accepted the challenge. I was scared a lot. I lived the whole year outside of my comfort zone. I stretched myself further than I wanted to reach, and then I overcame the resulting overwhelm. At times, I felt as though I was in over my head.

WHAT DID YOU LEARN ABOUT YOURSELF?

- *Resistance takes just as much work and energy as following through.*
- *Procrastination is, in effect, an escape from reality. It's an addictive behavior that needs to be treated and cured.*
- *If I want to be more productive, I have to spend more time producing and less time consuming.*
- *I have to know where I stand with people. If I can't tell who they are, what they value, if they like me, what they're thinking, etc.—the relationship quickly becomes toxic.*

WHO NURTURED AND SUPPORTED YOU?

- *My husband! I've always considered him extremely supportive, but man, he knocked it out of the ballpark this year*
- *My children—they're alert and looking for the good in life, and always generous with support*
- *My production assistant, Jennie—amazing! She matched my time spent on almost every project, and handles the club with respect*
- *My private clients and Luminaries—my goodness, how this group shines!*

WHO DID YOU ENJOY NURTURING AND SUPPORTING?

I was present and committed to contributing to my family's lives this year, they are always a priority. That said, I greatly enjoyed nurturing and supporting myself and my dreams. A lot of care and attention was invested inward, and I can't think of many years in my life where I've been so selfishly involved in my own affairs.

I wouldn't call what I did self-care or nurturing in the traditional sense, it was more a self-respect for my personal power and professionalism. I took myself and my endeavors quite seriously, and that's helped me come a long way.

what's not working?

WHAT WAS YOUR BIGGEST CHALLENGE THIS YEAR?

WHAT WILL YOU CHANGE GOING FORWARD?

WHAT WOULD (OR WOULDN'T) YOU CHANGE ABOUT HOW YOU HANDLED IT?

WHAT WAS MONEY WASTED?

DO YOU HAVE ANY UNFINISHED BUSINESS TO ATTEND TO?

example answers

WHAT WAS YOUR BIGGEST CHALLENGE THIS YEAR?

The hardest obstacle I tackled this year was facing uncertainty head on. I had to keep faith and calm my panic way more than I'd like to admit.

In taking myself more seriously this year, I also had to beware of taking myself too seriously. It seems a fine line to walk.

WHAT WILL YOU CHANGE GOING FORWARD?

I'm studying confidence-building to reduce self-doubt and social anxiety.

Mel Robbins' course for CreativeLive, How to Break the Habit of Self-Doubt and Build Real Confidence is an exceptional resource for this.

WHAT WOULD (OR WOULDN'T) YOU CHANGE ABOUT HOW YOU HANDLED IT?

I wouldn't have gotten so caught up in my head—things get very "doomsday" in there sometimes! I'm not entirely sure how to cure this, but I'm working on it.

My family could sense my stress this summer, and that's something I'd like to eliminate once and for all.

WHAT WAS MONEY WASTED?

- *PureBarre! Oh my gosh, what a ripoff. My local gym costs 1/4 of the monthly charges and offers similar classes.*
- *Webinar hosts! You name them, I've tried them—they're all junk this year.*
- *Business filing errors that cost me a fortune in taxes. I would have seen a substantial advantage had I seen an accountant sooner*

DO YOU HAVE ANY UNFINISHED BUSINESS TO ATTEND TO?

Yes. My year has been successful, but it's not over yet. To clear my plate for a productive 2018, I'd like to complete one more signature course, launch a podcast, and get ahead on my editorial calendar.

what's not working?

DO YOU HAVE ANY OUTSTANDING GOALS?

WHAT WAS YOUR WORST SETBACK?

DID YOU KEEP ANY BAD HABITS?

WHAT HELD YOU BACK?

HOW DID YOU HOLD YOURSELF BACK?

example answers

DO YOU HAVE ANY OUTSTANDING GOALS?

- *Do more live videos*
- *Schedule monthly dates with my husband*
- *Triple my website traffic*
- *Have my first six-figure month*
- *Hire more help*
- *Get back to the gym (3x week)*
- *Buy a new dining room table*
- *Book our next two dream vacations*

DID YOU KEEP ANY BAD HABITS?

My worst habit is mindless internet clicking—I do it as a form of procrastination.

Another struggle I have is overindulging in food or alcohol as a reward for a job well done (which sometimes leads to the undoing of the good deed).

WHAT WAS YOUR WORST SETBACK?

My worst setback this year was the summer; there were times when I completely lost faith and perspective. I couldn't see the forrest for the trees.

Within a few months, I had ...

- *recently moved into a much more expensive area, and for the first time, we were relying equally on my "less reliable" income*
- *paid a giant tax bill that wiped our savings*
- *lost the financial security we'd built just before the summer slow months hit*
- *taken big risks in upgrades and investments*

WHAT HELD YOU BACK?

Fear of loss, less, and never (Google Tony Robbins' view on the state of suffering).

HOW DID YOU HOLD YOURSELF BACK?

Anytime I feared the vision instead of acting upon it, I got stuck in my own way.

time management

TIME IS THE MOST PRECIOUS RESOURCE YOU HAVE ON EARTH, AND THE MAJORITY OF PEOPLE ARE WASTING IT. KNOW THE VALUE IN EACH OF YOUR 24 HOURS EVERY DAY. CREATE A PRACTICE OF ASKING YOURSELF: IF THIS MOMENT WERE A DOLLAR, AM I INVESTING IT OR BURNING IT?

WHAT ARE YOUR MAIN PRIORITIES IN LIFE?
LIST THEM IN ORDER OF IMPORTANCE.

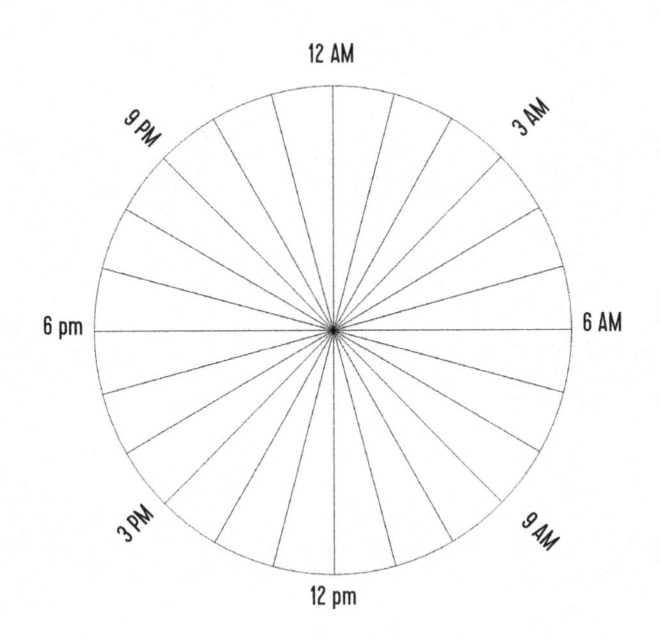

USE THE GRAPH TO CHART HOW YOU INVEST TIME DURING A TYPICAL 24-HOUR WEEKDAY.

DOES YOUR CHART REFLECT YOUR LIST OF PRIORITIES?
HOW MIGHT YOU REARRANGE YOUR SCHEDULE FOR BETTER RESULTS?

example answers

TIME IS THE MOST PRECIOUS RESOURCE YOU HAVE ON EARTH, AND THE MAJORITY OF PEOPLE ARE WASTING IT. KNOW THE VALUE IN EACH OF YOUR 24 HOURS EVERY DAY. CREATE A PRACTICE OF ASKING YOURSELF: IF THIS MOMENT WERE A DOLLAR, AM I INVESTING IT OR BURNING IT?

WHAT ARE YOUR MAIN PRIORITIES IN LIFE? LIST THEM IN ORDER OF IMPORTANCE.

1. *My five: my husband and children*
2. *Self-improvement*
3. *Fitness and health*
4. *Friendships and community*

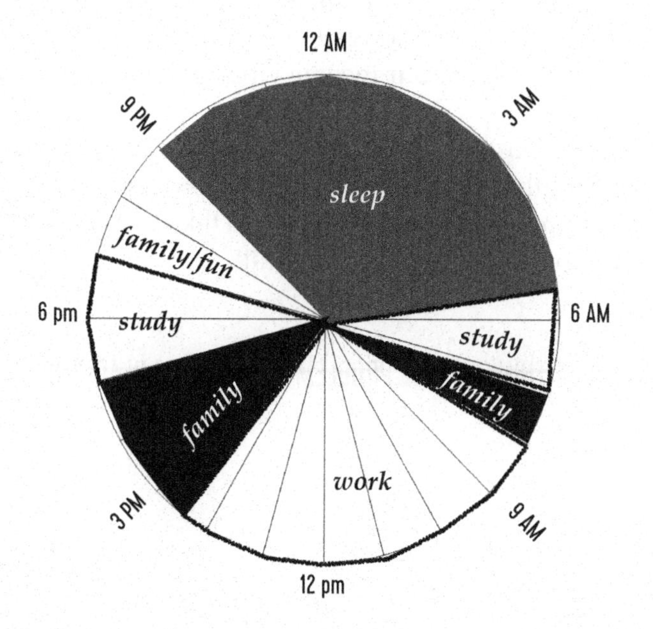

USE THE GRAPH TO CHART HOW YOU INVEST TIME DURING A TYPICAL 24-HOUR WEEKDAY.

DOES YOUR CHART REFLECT YOUR LIST OF PRIORITIES? HOW MIGHT YOU REARRANGE YOUR SCHEDULE FOR BETTER RESULTS?

I did this exercise last year and changed a lot about my day. I'm still following the same schedule and routine I set in Your Best Year 2017, and it serves me well. Going forward, I would like to allot more time for fitness and health in my daily routine.

Why Aren't You Rich Yet?

In one of my favorite books, *The Instant Millionaire: A Tale of Wisdom and Wealth* by Mark Fisher, a wise old millionaire asks a struggling young man, "How is it that you aren't rich yet? Have you ever seriously asked yourself that question?"

What an interesting perspective it brings! I love to introduce that line of questioning to any goal. Think of all the achievements you've struggled with in the past, and now ask yourself:

WHY HAVEN'T YOU FIXED IT YET?

- Why aren't you at your ideal weight yet?
- Why haven't you reached your sales goals yet?
- Why haven't you finished the project yet?
- Why isn't your relationship healthy yet?
- Why isn't your income what you think it should be yet?

Every obstacle in your way, every problem left unsolved, and every weakness that still needs strengthened is revealed in the answers to these questions. Let's face it, we act like spoiled children sometimes, refusing to take responsibility and rebelling against our own best intentions. It happens to us all!

THINK OF ONE PROBLEM THAT'S BEEN PLAGUING YOU FOR ENTIRELY TOO LONG. WRITE IT HERE.

IN WHAT AREAS DO YOU SUCCUMB TO INSTANT GRATIFICATION, THEREBY FOREGOING LONG-TERM GAIN?

SURVEY THE LAND

Land surveyors lay points on the terrain and determine the distances between them. Those measurements are then used to establish maps, which of course help people get to where they're going.

This section is designed to help you measure the distance between where you are and where you want to be. We'll use the rest of the book to build a map to get you there.

Let's imagine that you've just made an appointment with a world-class business mogul, and that meeting is scheduled exactly one month from today. She's interested to see what you're working on, and in exchange for her time and advice, you need to present everything you have so far (website, blog, social media, storefront, etc.).

- What would you do to prepare your presentation?
- Which parts of your business would you be ashamed to share?
- What would you frantically try to correct before the meeting?
- How would you package your skill set to make it even more appealing?

There are nagging tasks that each of us knows we should be doing, but we haven't taken action on them. Either you're just plain scared to invest or you're stalled in the face of overwhelm and uncertainty. But the truth is, most of us know *exactly* what we need to do next … we're simply not doing it.

"BEING BUSY IS A FORM OF LAZINESS—LAZY THINKING AND INDISCRIMINATE ACTION."—*Tim Ferriss*

More importantly, when you know you should be taking action, what do you do instead? What's your go-to procrastination technique? Mine's clicking on the internet, and because you're in online business, I'll bet you can relate.

Mindless clicking is a hazard of the job. It's certainly not productive, and would we even call it fun? No! It's pure avoidance. That clicking loop (Facebook, Pinterest, email, Instagram, email, Facebook, etc.) is ruthlessly sucking energy from your day and stealing time from your life.

Many of us will find that we give precious time to wasteful internet consumption in our morning routines, in waiting rooms, at red lights, and even during quality time with loved ones. We're conditioned to do it, but it's time to question that conditioning.

None of us—not one!—are going to get to the end of our lives and say, "I wish I would've replied to more emails." That's a fact that we can all agree to, but *how we want to spend our lives* and *where we invest time each day* are often a paradox.

survey the land

ARE YOU ATTRACTING NEW POTENTIAL CUSTOMERS ON A REGULAR BASIS?

DO YOU SHOW UP FOR YOUR BUSINESS EVERY DAY, WITHOUT FAIL?

WHAT'S LACKING ABOUT YOUR PRESENTATION?

ARE YOU A RELIABLE AND PRODUCTIVE EMPLOYEE?

WHAT DO YOU NEED TO IMPROVE IN ORDER TO BE THE TOP DOG IN YOUR INDUSTRY?

example answers

ARE YOU ATTRACTING NEW POTENTIAL CUSTOMERS ON A REGULAR BASIS?

No! This is the danger of going too inward on your work routine. This year, I finished a ton of new projects, but when I resurfaced after months of working privately, no one was around!

It's why I added this line of questioning, so you'll get the full scope of what you need to be doing for your business year-round.

DO YOU SHOW UP FOR YOUR BUSINESS EVERY DAY, WITHOUT FAIL?

I do, but there's always room for improvement.

WHAT'S LACKING ABOUT YOUR PRESENTATION?

A way for people to arrive and instantly connect.

Everything's part of a system in my business—blog points to email, email points to membership, etc. I realized I needed a way for people to land on my site and instantly connect in a meaningful way.

To cure this, I created a free three-part video training, Become a Best-Selling Strategist.

ARE YOU A RELIABLE AND PRODUCTIVE EMPLOYEE?

I am, but there must be a strict deadline and added accountability in play.

WHAT DO YOU NEED TO IMPROVE IN ORDER TO BE THE TOP DOG IN YOUR INDUSTRY?

Good question! I need to re-strategize my outreach program. Things change fast in online business, and what was working beautifully for years (Pinterest) is suddenly failing miserably. I haven't found the traffic source that can replace this. I'm not sure what the answer is, but I'll have it figured out soon.

I'm also going to create more ways for new visitors to instantly connect in meaningful ways by doing more live videos and film.

Last but not least, I need to showcase more of the Luminaries' results. The proof is in the pudding!

survey the land

DO YOU MAKE THE TOUGH DECISIONS THAT WILL ENSURE YOUR BUSINESS' SURVIVAL?

HAVE YOU BEEN COMFORTABLE WITH SUFFERING SOME DISCOMFORT?

ARE YOU A GOOD CEO? DO YOU SET TARGETS AND ACHIEVE COMPANY GOALS?

DO YOU KNOW WHAT THE MOST IMPORTANT TASKS ARE EACH DAY?

DO YOU CROSS THE IMPORTANT TASKS OFF YOUR TO-DO LIST EACH AND EVERY DAY?

example answers

DO YOU MAKE THE TOUGH DECISIONS THAT WILL ENSURE YOUR BUSINESS' SURVIVAL?

Yes. I make decisions quickly and second-guess myself much less than ever before.

If I need more information or input before I can make a decision, I set a deadline for when the matter must be decided.

HAVE YOU BEEN COMFORTABLE WITH SUFFERING SOME DISCOMFORT?

No, but I tackle it anyway! There's only so much uncertainty I care to handle at any given time, so feeling unsure about personal finances at the same time I was taking business risks was extremely uncomfortable for me this year.

I've learned a lot in the process. I've reorganized my goals to keep things settled and secure at home, so I can take even bigger risks in business!

ARE YOU A GOOD CEO? DO YOU SET TARGETS AND ACHIEVE COMPANY GOALS?

I'm a good CEO, but I can get better. I'm guilty of losing sight of the targets and goals at times, so I'll need to find a way to keep the vision front and center.

DO YOU KNOW WHAT THE MOST IMPORTANT TASKS ARE EACH DAY?

Yes! The system I'm sharing with you in Your Best Year 2018 ensures I know exactly what I should be working on every day.

DO YOU CROSS THE IMPORTANT TASKS OFF YOUR TO-DO LIST EACH AND EVERY DAY?

Not always, but that's been a matter of pacing, not productivity. I often overestimate what I can get done in a day, which sends my entire plan askew. I plan to refine the pace in 2018.

survey the land

WHERE WOULD YOU LIKE TO SEE YOUR BUSINESS IN ONE YEAR?

PLEASE WRITE THIS ANSWER AGAIN, ON PAGES 58 & 65

WHERE WOULD YOU LIKE TO SEE YOUR BUSINESS IN THREE YEARS?

WHO IS YOUR PIE-IN-THE-SKY ROLE MODEL? WHO WOULD YOU PROFESSIONALLY TRADE PLACES WITH?

IF YOU KNEW YOU COULD NOT FAIL, WHAT WOULD YOU TRY THIS YEAR?

WHAT WOULD CHANGE ABOUT YOU, YOUR LIFE, AND YOUR BUSINESS SHOULD THESE ASPIRATIONS OCCUR?

example answers

WHERE WOULD YOU LIKE TO SEE YOUR BUSINESS IN ONE YEAR?

Your Best Year 2018 reaches #1 in its category on Amazon's best-sellers list, finding its way into the hands of 100,000 online entrepreneurs.

Within one year, the Luminaries Club™ welcomes an additional 1,000 members to our ranks.

My podcast earns tens of thousands subscribers.

WHERE WOULD YOU LIKE TO SEE YOUR BUSINESS IN THREE YEARS?

I'm financially free. Rather than working for the business, the business works for me.

I have a corporate venue—a creative's wonderland of possibility.

I travel more often and lead luxurious retreats and conferences on growth and achievement.

WHO IS YOUR PIE-IN-THE-SKY ROLE MODEL? WHO WOULD YOU PROFESSIONALLY TRADE PLACES WITH?

Mine's a mixture! I admire ...

- *Tony Robbins' lifestyle*
- *Mel Robbins' stage presence*
- *Joanna Gaines' creative opportunities*
- *Elon Musk's ingenuity*
- *Jeff Bezo's business savvy*
- *Louise Hay's healing heart*

IF YOU KNEW YOU COULD NOT FAIL, WHAT WOULD YOU TRY THIS YEAR?

If I knew I could not fail, I would ...

- *Do a world tour. I would take my show (and my family) on the road and host retreats in Canada, Costa Rica, Spain, Italy, Norway, Greece, and Bali.*
- *Open a corporate venue that helps creative entrepreneurs get more done professionally*

WHAT WOULD CHANGE ABOUT YOU, YOUR LIFE, AND YOUR BUSINESS SHOULD THESE ASPIRATIONS OCCUR?

I can only imagine how utterly fulfilling it would be to achieve such things. I say I'm glad I didn't quit because it begs the question: how much of myself would I have missed out on? This page makes me feel like: How much of myself is out there, still unrealized?

I would reach a level I never imagined was available to me.

create the vision

WHAT HAS TO HAPPEN IN 2018 FOR IT TO FEEL LIKE AN ABSOLUTE SUCCESS?

WHAT WILL BE DIFFERENT FOR YOU ONCE THE VISION IS REALIZED?

WHAT WILL YOU BE ABLE TO DO THEN THAT YOU CANNOT DO NOW?

WHAT WILL BE DIFFERENT FOR YOUR LOVED ONES ONCE THE VISION IS REALIZED?

WHAT ACTIONS DO YOU THINK WILL GET YOU THERE?

example answers

WHAT HAS TO HAPPEN IN 2018 FOR IT TO FEEL LIKE AN ABSOLUTE SUCCESS?

Significant growth and profit to include ...

- *a more diverse, more specially-trained support team*
- *outrageous growth—I would like to at least double my current list*
- *significant increase in revenue—I would like to at least double my current profits*

WHAT WILL BE DIFFERENT FOR YOU ONCE THE VISION IS REALIZED?

Debt will be paid down (or in full), reintroducing stability and security to my personal finances.

I'll have more fun mixed in and around all of the seriousness of going pro with my career.

WHAT WILL YOU BE ABLE TO DO THEN THAT YOU CANNOT DO NOW?

I'll be able to soar; work will be less of a grind. I'll be open to new creative opportunities (and have room in my schedule to actually accept them).

My business endeavors will enhance my life rather than detract from it.

WHAT WILL BE DIFFERENT FOR YOUR LOVED ONES ONCE THE VISION IS REALIZED?

Everyone's financial future becomes more secure once I achieve my goals—they'll have less student loans and more future support.

We'll be able to enjoy luxurious indulgences without the "how much does that cost?!" panic.

WHAT ACTIONS DO YOU THINK WILL GET YOU THERE?

- *More output overall, with more opt-in offers mixed in*
- *Maybe a medium buy-in price point (versus just low and high offers)*
- *More affiliates and more contests for them*
- *Another video sequence with an easy buy-in offer*

what do you want to change?

BEFORE YOU SET YOUR ANNUAL OBJECTIVES FOR THE YEAR AHEAD, CONSIDER THE FIVE PILLARS OF A HARMONIC LIFE, AS TAUGHT IN HARMONIC WEALTH: THE SECRET OF ATTRACTING THE LIFE YOU WANT BY JAMES ARTHUR RAY: (1) FINANCIAL, (2) SPIRITUAL, (3) MENTAL, (4) RELATIONAL, AND (5) PHYSICAL. WHEN PROMPTED, SUMMARIZE YOUR ANSWERS ON PAGE 91. WHAT WOULD YOU LIKE TO IMPROVE?

FINANCIAL:

SPIRITUAL:

MENTAL:

PHYSICAL:

RELATIONAL:

example answers

BEFORE YOU SET YOUR ANNUAL OBJECTIVES FOR THE YEAR AHEAD, CONSIDER THE FIVE PILLARS OF A HARMONIC LIFE, AS TAUGHT IN HARMONIC WEALTH: THE SECRET OF ATTRACTING THE LIFE YOU WANT BY JAMES ARTHUR RAY: (1) FINANCIAL, (2) SPIRITUAL, (3) MENTAL, (4) RELATIONAL, AND (5) PHYSICAL. WHAT WOULD YOU LIKE TO IMPROVE?

FINANCIAL: *I want to pay down debts and build up personal asset value. I'd like the business to see its first six-figure month. I'll continue to reserve operating expenses, possibly hire a bigger team, and bring home a net profit that helps us to never borrow (for house or otherwise) again.*

SPIRITUAL: *I would like to rise up out of the incidentals of life and enjoy the big picture. I want to be more present in every moment. I'd like to enjoy working, playing, and living to the fullest! I hope to find more peace through improved self-care and quiet rituals every day.*

MENTAL: *I will stay sharp and continue to study the subject matter that strengthens my weaknesses. I'll aim to do even more by way of learning and teaching this year. I'll seek out faster ways to produce and deliver big lessons.*

PHYSICAL: *The unnecessary weight is gone, and now it's time to get in shape and stick to a routine! I'll run for the love of it but strive to get back to the gym for classes and weights at least 5x week.*

RELATIONAL: *I'll continue to learn how to do what's best by my husband and children. I'll offer them a love they can count on and the space to grow beyond it. I'll look for more things we can do together as a unit and continue to honor the traditions we've created.*

Create a Visualization for Success

I don't share the details often, but I'm what people call "woo woo." I believe in energy, the law of attraction, a universal source, God, guides, and all things spiritual and loving. I treasure my oracle cards and honor my chakras. I'm open and receptive to all good (and that happens to be one of my favorite positive affirmations that I recite daily).

While that is my nature, I also operate with a healthy level of discernment. I thoroughly question everything before I throw my faith into it. My experience with visualizations was no different. But I thought, *what could it hurt?*

I love my life, but I wasn't necessarily happy when I did my first visualization exercise. In fact, I felt stuck, scared, and uncertain at the time. I wanted to feel better, and if imagining myself in a feel-better place might help, then I was willing to give it a try. And, it worked.

Everything I'd written down, every way I'd wished for my life to improve, came to fruition. So, of course I kept doing it! In 2013, I was able to document the results in an extraordinary way.

I was living in New Zealand at the time, and another huge relocation was on the horizon. It seemed like all my family did was move, and I wasn't the only one who was sick and tired of being uprooted. We all were.

My husband, children, and I desperately craved roots and a deep sense of belonging. We were starved for familiarity. We were headed back to Northern Virginia where it costs a mega-fortune to live in a nice neighborhood.

As we looked for the perfect house, my husband and I wound ourselves up into a constant state of low-grade panic. Our searches always made us feel like we were a million dollars short. We were mentally looping the issue, and things looked bleak. Uncertainty reared its ugly head.

That's when I decided to write a visualization for six months into the future. I got a brand new journal for Christmas, and on December 27, 2012, I made the first entry. I'm going to share a partial excerpt with you here.

Before I do, I need to tell you two things:

1. I had an internal debate about sharing this publicly, as my spirituality is such a personal and private part of my life. However, the results are so impressive that if it helps at least one person create positive change in their life, it will have been well worth it.
2. As much as I tried to convince myself with positive affirmations and an optimistic mindset, I did not believe any of the following visualization points would be in Virginia, in my price range, or at all possible.

I'm heading into 2013 with these top priorities [partial].

- *Provide comfort, care, and plenty of luxe for the children, my husband, and me. We've thoroughly enjoyed New Zealand and our time exploring the South Pacific. However, it's been a pretty cramped living situation and a long stretch from home. I'm ready to celebrate comfortable spaciousness in all aspects of our life.*
- *Love my neighborhood. It's really important that I feel safe and comfortable with where my children grow up. I'd also love for my husband and I to meet some great people and enjoy the community as well.*
- *Own land. I can't add it to the house later.*
- *Live in our dream house. It has 5+ bedrooms, at least 3 bathrooms, and a home office with French doors. It has a kitchen I can't take my eyes off of (in a good way) and 1-2 fireplaces (preferably wood-burning). It has a finished basement that my husband adores, a gorgeous flat lawn for the children to play in, and an in-ground swimming pool with a deep end that we all love. It's filled with light and character, good wine, and laughter. We six are head-over-heels in LOVE with the place. It's ours.*

Life got busy after that. In its entirety, that journal entry was four pages long and the only one in the book. When we moved, it got packed with my other belongings, and I didn't open it again until July 23, 2013.

This is what happened a few months later. In March of 2013, we closed on a house (in our price range!) that sat on a flat, gorgeous lawn—an acre of land. It had 5 bedrooms, 4.5 baths, a home office with a French door, a fireplace, an amazing kitchen and … (drumroll please) … an in-ground swimming pool with a deep end.

I became the social chairwoman for our neighborhood board—my husband and I met tons of people right away. My children had creeks and trails to explore within a gorgeous, safe area. In all scenarios, that visualization (or something better) manifested in my life.

Create a visualization of your own. Imagine six months into the future, and create the most ideal outcome for yourself. For relationships, describe how the people you're closest with are doing, and how you're relating to them. What are they experiencing and achieving? Imagine them fulfilling their passions while you discover yours, and how those relationships evolve.

Next, what are you doing, learning, reading, and enjoying? Describe your own evolution. Are you living up to your potential? Are you fit and active? Do you feel excited about your life? What about your environment? Does your home need to be redecorated, remodeled, or even relocated to another, more fitting location? If something's not working, imagine it better.

What would feel better for your personal finances? Debt is paid down, financial freedom is on the horizon, and out of the blue, you realized another source of income you earn while doing something you love! Get creative here, and imagine yourself prospering at every turn.

What about the rest of the world? How do they receive you when they see you? How do you get along with your co-workers? How has your difficult family member become a little easier to get along with? Imagine all of the people outside of your inner circle, and write down where you'd like the relationships to go.

visualization

IN SIX MONTHS, MY RELATIONSHIPS ARE ....

I AM ...

MY HOME IS ...

MY FINANCES ...

MY EXTENDED FAMILY AND FRIENDS ...

example answers

IN SIX MONTHS, MY RELATIONSHIPS ARE ....

easy, clean, and whole. My family continues to explore the world together, while giving each member the trust and freedom to define their own route. My marriage is thriving; our love is strong, supportive, and secure. My children are happy; they feel comfortable, respected, and treasured.

I AM ...

alive! I've conquered fear and self-doubt, and I've grown into the woman I was always meant to be. I wear a cloak of power and glory. I'm comfortable with myself, and that makes others incredibly comfortable around me. I have a deep sense of belonging, and that helps me to fit in and make friends wherever I go.

MY HOME IS ...

completely my own. We've made the updates and additions so that this cozy little house fits us like a glove. I wake up and go to sleep in the bedroom of my dreams, my children have rooms that reflect their personalities, my husband has the basement he's always dreamed of, and we're in the process of putting in the screened porch I've always wanted.

MY FINANCES ...

have hit the fast lane, and we make responsible choices to secure our future and seal our good financial fate. We're entirely debt-free and on our way to passive rental income, treasuries, and municipal bonds.

MY EXTENDED FAMILY AND FRIENDS ...

offer healthy and strong connections. I'm surrounded by women who nurture clean bonds and good friendships. My family loves embarking on new adventures with treasured friends.

next level list

WHAT DO YOU NEED TO DO TO NEXT LEVEL?

BY:

BY:

BY:

BY:

BY:

BY:

BY:

BY:

This is the most important question in the book. These things you've written? They're *a lot of work,* and I commend you for being brave enough to write down the things that challenge you.

In fact, you've already done more than most! Think of this as a mental head start. You can do all of these things on your list; they're 100% doable. Is it going to be easy? No. Comfort is easy. Complaining is easy. Constant low-grade dissatisfaction with your life is easy *and* common. The next level is uncommon and extraordinary. You're already on your way.

example answers

WHAT DO YOU NEED TO DO TO NEXT LEVEL?

Finish and launch new course, Shop 2.0

BY: *January*

List 2 courses on Skillshare

BY: *February*

Editorial calendar running 3 months in advance

BY: *February*

Best-Selling Strategist > Evergreen campaign

BY: *February*

Find or accept 3 all-new speaking gigs

BY: *July*

Launch Your Best Year 2019

BY: *October*

Create self-hosted sales pages

BY: *October*

Hire club counselors for the Luminaries Club™

BY: *November*

THINGS I DID IN 2017

More example things I did in 2017: hired full-time support, hired part-time support, invested in custom brand and web design, hired a professional photographer, invested in preventative legal, created an affiliate program, created an opt-in video training, and started a podcast.

what are you afraid of?

WHAT FEARS ARE HOLDING YOU BACK? LIST THEM ALL, WHETHER YOU CONSIDER THEM RATIONAL OR NOT.

WORLD FAMOUS AUTHOR AND ENTREPRENEUR, TIM FERRISS RECOMMENDS AN EXERCISE CALLED "FEAR-SETTING." IT'S SOMETHING HE DOES AT LEAST QUARTERLY. THE IDEA BEING THAT, IN ORDER TO CONQUER FEAR, YOU MUST DEFINE IT FIRST. ONCE YOUR FEARS ARE NAMED, YOU THEN FIGURE OUT THE WORST THING THAT COULD HAPPEN SHOULD ANY OF THEM ACTUALLY HAPPEN.

ON A SCALE OF 1—10, 1 BEING CALM AND 10 BEING FULL-BLOWN PANIC, HOW SCARED ARE YOU OF EACH FEAR?

ON A SCALE OF 1—10, 1 BEING NO BIG DEAL AND 10 BEING A LIFE-CHANGING AND PERMANENT DISASTER, HOW BADLY WOULD ANY OF THESE FEARS COMING TO FRUITION AFFECT YOUR LIFE?

example answers

WHAT FEARS ARE HOLDING YOU BACK? LIST THEM ALL, WHETHER YOU CONSIDER THEM RATIONAL OR NOT.

- *My business will run out of money, I won't get paid, and I'll be forced to dip into personal finances. I'll jeopardize my family's security.*

    How scared am I? 8
    Worst case scenario: We downsize, reduce extra costs, and I get a job
    How scary is that, actually? 2

- *Business will dry up, and I'll have wasted ten years investing into a career that no longer exists!*

    How scared am I? 5
    Worst case scenario: It's been a wild ride while it lasted. What can I do next?
    How scary is that, actually? 2

- *Nobody buys my next product or books tickets to my next event (that I've already invested tons of money and time into).*

    How scared am I? 6
    Worst case scenario: I have something to add to my portfolio of offers or a paid-for party with my friends
    How scary is that, actually? 0

Naming and ranking my fears helped me put things into perspective this year. *I had a lot of deadlines. Worst case, I'd have to pull a few all-nighters. And that's not a life changing disaster! It's just one year of tight deadlines, and that could be noted and improved on the following year.*

THE REASONS WHY

This is the most important section of the book. Why? Because you've got to take action every day, but it won't be every day that you actually see results. The only thing that's certain is that you're going to face uncertainty. You'll have to battle fear, doubt, and insecurity along the way. You'll need constant ammunition (in the form of motivation).

You need something you can have control over, and this is it. Your reasons *why.*

And I mean very selfishly, why? When I ask my private clients to tell me why they want the success they crave, they fire off a list of logical answers:

- I want to save for retirement.
- I want to be able to pay my bills with ease.
- I would like to become debt-free.
- I want to serve people and make their lives better.
- I want to help others achieve their goals.
- I want to make good art.
- I want to provide valuable resources.
- I want to pursue a higher calling.
- I want to donate more to charity and causes I believe in.

I don't doubt any of these are true, they're each very logical and good. It's a well-thought out list; all great plans for the future.

However, we can't live a life and career of *giving* without creating some gleefully *selfish* rewards. And when I say gleefully selfish, I mean the kind of rewards that make you break out in spontaneous dance moves, hoots, whoops, and hollers even thinking about them (regardless of where you are and who's watching).

When was the last time you did that?! We all need more unadulterated glee in our lives!

I want to strip you of the very natural human need for instant gratification, but not to leave you drought and barren. If you take out instant gratification without adding in rewards, it's a recipe for misery and failure.

All actions are born of emotional desire. If you take action to lose weight, it's typically not because you know it would be healthier for your heart if you did so (logical thinking). People lose weight because they want to look better in their clothes, show up better in their lives, and live longer for the people they love (emotional desire).

If you take action and buy a product, it's generally not because you've measured the cost versus the gain and value (logical thinking). People buy because they want to increase their status, improve their lifestyle, or enhance their quality of life (emotional desire).

If you take action on your new goals, it will not be because there's a retirement plan you can't wait to contribute to (logical thinking). The only way to take action on your future goals *consistently* is to line up highly desirable rewards you can take steps toward today. You must attach emotional rewards that involve anticipation, excitement, and exhilaration to your goals in order to achieve them.

Why? Because emotional desire ignites motivation. Desire lights the fire beneath you, and it's the only thing that keeps the flame going long after the initial excitement for the goal has passed. That's why you need very selfish reasons why, *in addition to* all of the logical things you can do to contribute to your long-term success.

For example, if I meet my end-year business goals, I'm taking my family on an obscenely luxurious vacation. I've got a family of six, and I'm tired of schlepping around the country based on what we can afford.

If I meet my dreamiest goals this year, we will travel like the world's rich and famous. We'll fly first class to the best Caribbean island where we'll stay in a fully-staffed villa on the beach.

YES! That's what gets me jumping out of bed in the morning! That's what makes me start my timer, work my powerblocks, and bang my best content out *when I'd rather do anything else*. Let my competition click around on Facebook and procrastinate away their day! I'm busy writing my next best-seller because I need to make it RAIN. Turks and Caicos, here I come!

Champions persist because they never take their eye off the prize. Not only do entrepreneurs fail to keep focus, they forget to designate a prize and a finish line! You need both, or you'll lose the fire and drive it takes to keep your engine running.

"COMMITMENT IS DOING THE THING YOU SAID YOU WERE GOING TO DO LONG AFTER THE MOOD YOU SAID IT IN HAS LEFT YOU."—Darren Hardy

The huge reward you set will be even more motivating if you make incremental deposits toward it. Let's say your reward is a luxury vacation to white sandy beaches and clear waters. You may not have money for the whole trip, but you can start with a new bathing suit. You can apply for your passport. You can get a beach bag, and block the dates on your calendar. You can book the airline tickets, then the place to stay, and before you know it, you'll be on your way!

reasons why

THE VISION FOR 2018 [COPIED FROM PAGE 42]

WHAT WILL I DO FOR MY FUTURE WHEN I ACHIEVE THIS GOAL?

WHAT RIDICULOUSLY EXTRAVAGANT GIFT WILL I REWARD MYSELF IF I ACHIEVE THIS VISION?

WHAT WILL BE BETTER ABOUT MY LIFE THEN THAT I FEEL MIGHT BE LACKING NOW?

AFTER I'VE ACHIEVED THIS, WHAT'S THE NEXT GOAL I'LL SET TO IMPROVE MY LIFE AND BUSINESS?

example answers

THE VISION FOR 2018 [COPIED FROM PAGE 43]

Your Best Year 2018 reaches #1 in its category on Amazon's best-sellers list, finding its way into the hands of 100,000 online entrepreneurs.

Within one year, the Luminaries Club™ welcomes an additional 1,000 members to our ranks.

My podcast earns tens of thousands subscribers.

WHAT WILL I DO FOR MY FUTURE WHEN I ACHIEVE THIS GOAL?

- *Pay off mortgage*
- *Set aside money for kids' college*
- *Create savings toward future investments*

WHAT RIDICULOUSLY EXTRAVAGANT GIFT WILL I REWARD MYSELF IF I ACHIEVE THIS VISION?

Our favorite: a Disney Cruise!

WHAT WILL BE BETTER ABOUT MY LIFE THEN THAT I FEEL MIGHT BE LACKING NOW?

- *I'll break out of the consumer cycle (more lending, less borrowing)*
- *Let my business take all the risks*
- *Have a more secure plan for the future*

AFTER I'VE ACHIEVED THIS, WHAT'S THE NEXT GOAL I'LL SET TO IMPROVE MY LIFE AND BUSINESS?

- *Invest in rental property*

BUILD AN ANNUAL STRATEGY

The plan inside *Your Best Year* is designed around the upcoming twelve months and your business' strongest season. This strategy enables you to keep your priorities in order of importance: your life, *then* your business. It will not only help you eliminate the daily scramble, it also guarantees you'll improve your results and enhance your career.

First, look at the coming year and identify where you will need time off, such as summer vacation, winter holidays, important dates, back to school, etc. List these special events on your calendar before listing business-related projects or promotions.

In the example exercise, I've noted all of my personal time with a star.★

JANUARY	FEBRUARY	MARCH	APRIL
	★ *weekend getaway*	★ *spring break*	

MAY	JUNE	JULY	AUGUST
	★ *summer vacation*		★ *weekend getaway* ★ *back to school*

SEPTEMBER	OCTOBER	NOVEMBER	DECEMBER
	★ *weekend getaway*		★ *downtime*

I'm not out of the game where you see personal notations, but it is still important to bring awareness to the events to ensure I leave plenty of space for them.

For example, I tend to go stir-crazy in February, and it messes with my emotions and my outlook. I made note to plan a long weekend away that month. I also write down quotes that are very meaningful, so I can refer back to them the following year in the same season, such as this great reminder for February and summer months alike!

"DON'T DIG UP IN DOUBT WHAT YOU PLANTED IN FAITH."—*Elizabeth Elliot*

Notice that personal occasions are on the calendar long before any product or promotional launches, and you can see my year already starting to take shape. I'm obviously not going to launch a new course or host a busy promotion in December (or worse, as a last-minute scramble for business) because I've already claimed white space in my calendar that month. I can set up the rest of the year to ensure I get time off.

I'm always looking for ways to improve my work-life flow. When I notice something I love or dislike about my schedule, I take note. Some examples are:

- No more projects that drag on longer than three months
- Tons of energy this month—do work!
- Need a break this time of year, schedule regular self-care
- Planning too much for one quarter, add margin
- Missing family, schedule more downtime this month
- Increasingly anxious here, find a cure

Strive to constantly gain more intel on your routine and schedule. The creative energy you spend in this business is an expensive fuel to burn. If you don't bring awareness to and continually replenish that energy, you'll quickly run out of gas and fail to meet your goals.

The next thing you're going to add to your calendar is your busier seasons. If you have an existing business, you can check your annual statistics for the months where you get most traffic. If not, you can use my examples as a guide.

It is the nature of business to have hot and cold seasons, most do. This technique is in place to help you utilize those seasons to their fullest. For example, it seems like everyone is on the internet in January, whereas in February, nobody's online. There will be plenty of average months in between, but it's important to take note of the high and low tides in particular. I've noted seasons with a bullet. ●

JANUARY	FEBRUARY	MARCH	APRIL
● *everybody > internet*	★ *weekend getaway* ● *nobody > internet*	★ *spring break*	
MAY	**JUNE**	**JULY**	**AUGUST**
	★ *summer vacation*	● *nobody > internet*	★ *weekend getaway* ★ *back to school*
SEPTEMBER	**OCTOBER**	**NOVEMBER**	**DECEMBER**
	★ *weekend getaway*	● *everybody > internet*	★ *downtime*

Moneymakers

With full awareness of your personal schedule, as well as busy and slow seasons, it is time to plug in the moneymakers. There are many different ways your business can earn money, but I'm going to advise you to specifically name three to six moneymakers. These will be the larger promotions or projects that anchor your entire year.

When scheduling your moneymakers, you'll want to avoid the slow seasons and steer clear of your personal occasions. Here is an example of a service-based business (my blog is the point of sale). Moneymakers are noted with an arrow.➡

JANUARY	FEBRUARY	MARCH	APRIL
● *everybody > internet* ➡ *new course*	★ *weekend getaway* ● *nobody > internet*	★ *spring break*	➡ *new book*
MAY	**JUNE**	**JULY**	**AUGUST**
➡ *Luminaries enrollment*	★ *summer vacation*	● *nobody > internet*	★ *weekend getaway* ★ *back to school*
SEPTEMBER	**OCTOBER**	**NOVEMBER**	**DECEMBER**
➡ *Luminaries price increase*	★ *weekend getaway* ➡ *Your Best Year 2019*	● *everybody > internet*	★ *downtime*

So much is revealed when big projects are added to the annual calendar. Rather than be stifled by the slow seasons, you can use them to your advantage. You can start prepping, promoting, and creating excitement around the next big event. You can make your best seasons even better. With this big picture in mind, you will know when your efforts will be rewarded.

This calendar will also help you to determine when to stock up on inventory, when to work ahead, when to take a break, and so on and so forth. *Your Best Year* is designed to help you pinpoint <u>what</u> to work on, this annual strategy helps you define <u>when</u>.

Your business rises and falls according to the effort you invest. When you know your seasons, you can create your own peaks and crest rather than become victim to them.

Use the form on the next page to plug in your personal time, seasonal tides, and moneymakers.

YOUR ANNUAL STRATEGY

JANUARY	FEBRUARY	MARCH	APRIL

MAY	JUNE	JULY	AUGUST

SEPTEMBER	OCTOBER	NOVEMBER	DECEMBER

1. *Add your personal and life occasions*
2. *Add seasonal highs and lows*
3. *Add the main moneymakers for the year*

How to Reach Your Goals

As I've mentioned, you will need to do four specific things to reach your goals and beyond this year. You'll need to make …

- your goals resolute,
- your strategies specific,
- your system efficient, and
- your action plan productive.

Let's talk about how to maximize return on your working hours and crush your business goals this year. With months of potential ahead and a long list of goals to achieve, you probably feel a panicked urgency to get #allthethings done RIGHT NOW. That's normal.

New Year energy is extremely frenetic, meaning it's hyperactive, unruly and wild. It's fueled by the unlimited potential we see in the clean slate of a fresh calendar. While there's a lot of good intention behind it, that energy has a short life span and quickly feels more agitating than motivating.

This is the reason January sees a huge increase in sales on fitness equipment, gym memberships, and diet programs. We are all looking to better our lives in a fevered way, but because this energy is so impatient, 95% of people give up within a few weeks.

I'm here to ensure you are not one of them.

And by the way, this isn't even about January 1. This cycle of energetic motivation is actually a quarterly thing. You'll feel a similar energy at the start of each season, but it is definitely at its peak when you're ringing in the New Year.

Remember, this is about the long game. Make a commitment to lasting success. Don't overestimate what you can do in a day, a week, or even a year. Stop, reevaluate, and reset when necessary. Aim for small, consistent improvements.

"SETTING GOALS IS THE FIRST STEP IN TURNING THE INVISIBLE INTO THE VISIBLE."—Tony Robbins

getting your goals

THE VISION FOR 2018 (COPIED FROM PAGE 42):

HOW MANY TIMES HAVE YOU TRIED AND FAILED TO ACHIEVE THE RESULTS YOU WANT?

WHEN YOU'RE **NOT** ACTIVELY WORKING TOWARD THE GOAL, WHAT DO YOU DO INSTEAD?

APPROXIMATELY HOW LONG WOULD YOU NEED TO FOREGO THE ABOVE ACTIVITIES AND REPLACE THEM WITH A BETTER HABIT BEFORE YOU WOULD SEE RESULTS?

WHAT'S THE FIRST SMALL CHANGE YOU CAN MAKE TO YOUR SCHEDULE?

WHAT'S A REASONABLE END DATE TO ACHIEVE THE DESIRED GOAL?

I'LL START ______________________ AND HAVE IT FINISHED BY ______________

THE VISION FOR 2018 (COPIED FROM PAGE 43):

Your Best Year 2018 reaches #1 in its category on Amazon's best-sellers list, finding its way into the hands of 100,000 online entrepreneurs. Within one year, the Luminaries Club™ welcomes an additional 1,000 members to our ranks. My podcast earns tens of thousands subscribers.

HOW MANY TIMES HAVE YOU TRIED AND FAILED TO ACHIEVE THE RESULTS YOU WANT?

I've tried to focus on membership goals for about three years, but I often get sidetracked and end up working on other things. This will be the second year I attack this specific goal.

WHEN YOU'RE NOT ACTIVELY WORKING TOWARD THE GOAL, WHAT DO YOU DO INSTEAD?

I get lost in the hustle and lose my way. Then, when I feel overwhelmed, I mindlessly click-loop on the internet or add unnecessary extra research into early stages of production. I put off the first action steps.

APPROXIMATELY HOW LONG WOULD YOU NEED TO FOREGO THE ABOVE ACTIVITIES AND REPLACE THEM WITH A BETTER HABIT BEFORE YOU WOULD SEE RESULTS?

If I stop thinking about my to-do list and set an intention to cross things off of it instead, I see better results within days.

WHAT'S THE FIRST SMALL CHANGE YOU CAN MAKE TO YOUR SCHEDULE?

I can do something more productive offline after my morning powerblocks are completed. My creative energy is at its lowest in the afternoon, so I find myself clicking instead of producing. I could workout instead, or leave time for admin and strategy there (easy/fun things for me).

WHAT'S A REASONABLE END DATE TO ACHIEVE THE DESIRED GOAL?

Ten months

I'LL START *now* **AND HAVE IT FINISHED BY** *October 31, 2018*

YOUR BEST YEAR PLAN

So far, we've covered the current **status** of your business to include your odds of getting ahead, a survey of the land, and a state of the union on your current conditions.

We then covered the hidden **desire** behind the results you crave to include your emotional outcomes and selfish reasons why.

It's now time to form the **strategy** for your year to include how you'll tackle the obstacles ahead, how you'll get what you set out to achieve, and how to find a pace that builds both the rhythm and momentum required.

Following my plan, you'll never wonder what you should be working on again. Here's a complete look at the system.

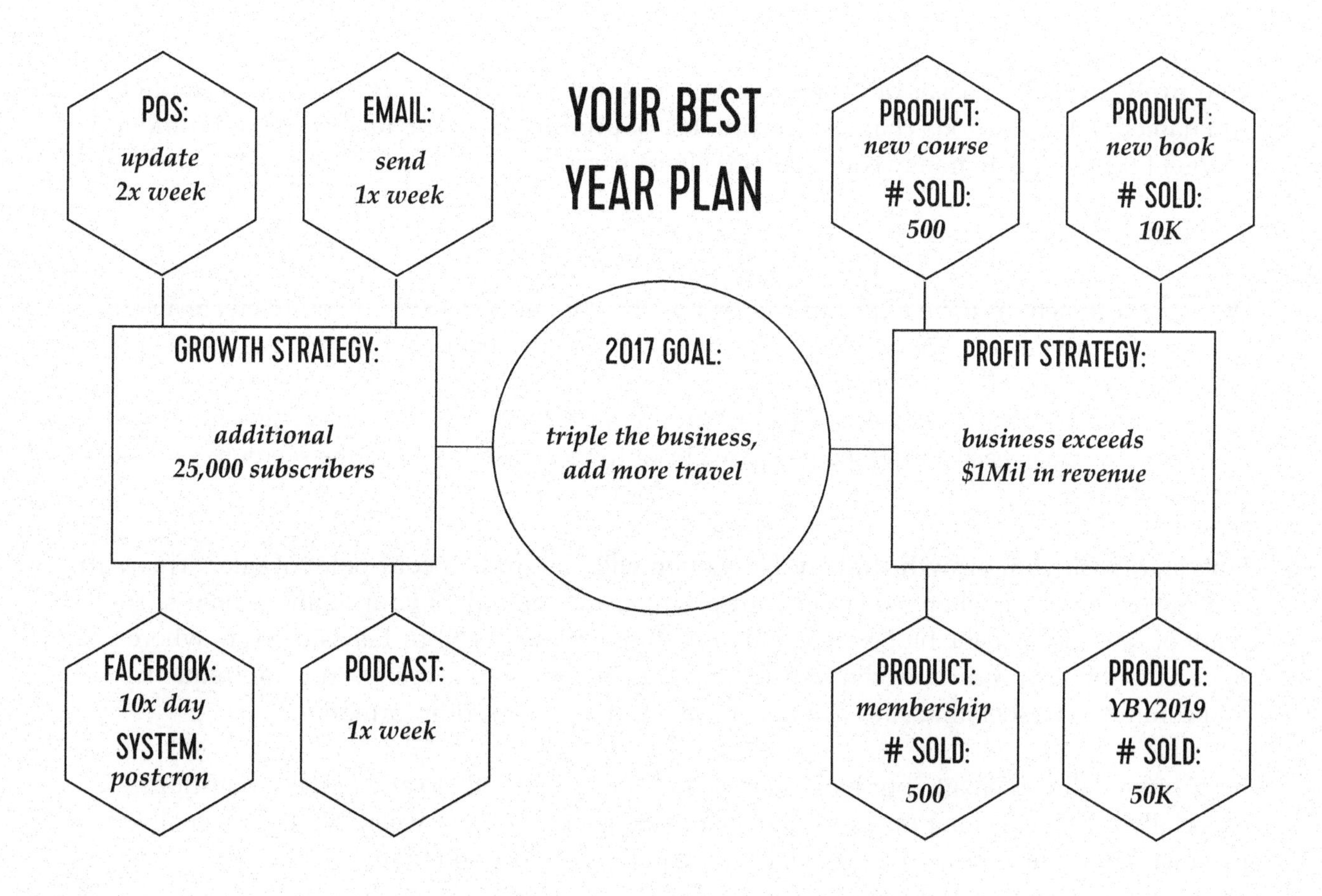

Your goal should always result in growth or profit, and preferably both. One usually feeds the other: growth brings more profit, and more profit brings faster growth.

In the graphic on the previous page, every activity has a purpose. Every moneymaker has a target. Notice how smaller activities always funnel into a larger strategy, and they're systemized where possible. Each activity on the chart ultimately feeds the goal.

Anytime you start fussing over your schedule or looming to-do list, I want you to question what you're doing, and more importantly, WHY you're doing it.

The Strategies

Once you have set a goal that you are determined to reach, you need to develop the strategies that will help you achieve it. The strategies are divided into our two main categories: growth and profit.

Your **growth strategy** consists of all the places you build and market your business online: your website or storefront (POS = point of sale), your email list, and two to three social media platforms where you reach and connect with your ideal customers. The systems are what automates as much of these activities as possible, such as Postcron (my favorite social media scheduler).

Your **profit strategy** consists of the moneymakers (three to six annual products or promotions) you named in the previous chapter. The number of products sold for any launch or promotion is a target for how much money could potentially be earned.

The Action Plan

We want your actions to be as productive as possible, so before I send you off to create a plan, let's assess your current operation. With your vision for 2018 front and center, ask yourself what activities you are willing to commit to all year in order to achieve it. Your challenge is going to be to continuously move the needle toward progress even when you're not getting immediate results. Remember, each small step gets you closer to the finish line, and the secret to success is completion.

Let's start with your growth strategy. How often will you update your point of sale? This is the website or storefront where you offer your product, and the hub of your online business. Your point of sale could be the blog where you offer digital products, your Etsy storefront where you offer a handmade product, or the website that houses something similar. At what frequency will you commit to freshen that site with new products, blog posts, or information?

How often will you email your list? There is no "one size fits all" to any of these questions, especially this one. I email my blog readers an average of once per week, but I only emailed my product-based business an average eight times per year. It doesn't matter the frequency you choose, but do commit to a routine.

Which social media platforms do you not only reach out, but also connect and engage with followers? Most successful online business owners dominate one or two social media platforms (not all). I advise my clients to avoid being everywhere, connecting with no one. Instead, pick your two most successful platforms and focus on enhancing your presence there.

Finally, how can you make your operation more efficient? Look for systems that will automate your workflow so you don't have to touch or "check it" every day. Which tasks can be batched, scheduled ahead, or outsourced?

Your growth strategy will require time, training, practice, patience, and small investments in scheduling software, but it will all pay off exponentially.

Next, look at your profit strategy. This consists of products or promotions (your three to six moneymakers) for the year. You want to list each moneymaker, how much you'll charge (or average sale amount, if it's a product promotion), and then write a target for how much money could potentially be earned. This will help you project whether or not the moneymakers will add up to the desired income goal, after taxes and expenses are deducted.

You'll also be prompted to name a release date for each product. I like to spread my major promotions out, leaving eight to twelve weeks between the next big sale. Here again, there's no "one size fits all." You know the seasons of your business better than anyone.

Your profit strategy requires traffic (online visitors), planning, training, copywriting, marketing, and later, an investment in advertising. Because once you have a working system in place, more traffic is the easiest part! Traffic is for sale; you can buy it anytime.

The following plan ensures that each activity feeds the goal and keeps your operation running like a well-oiled machine. It's time to plan your best year.

your best year

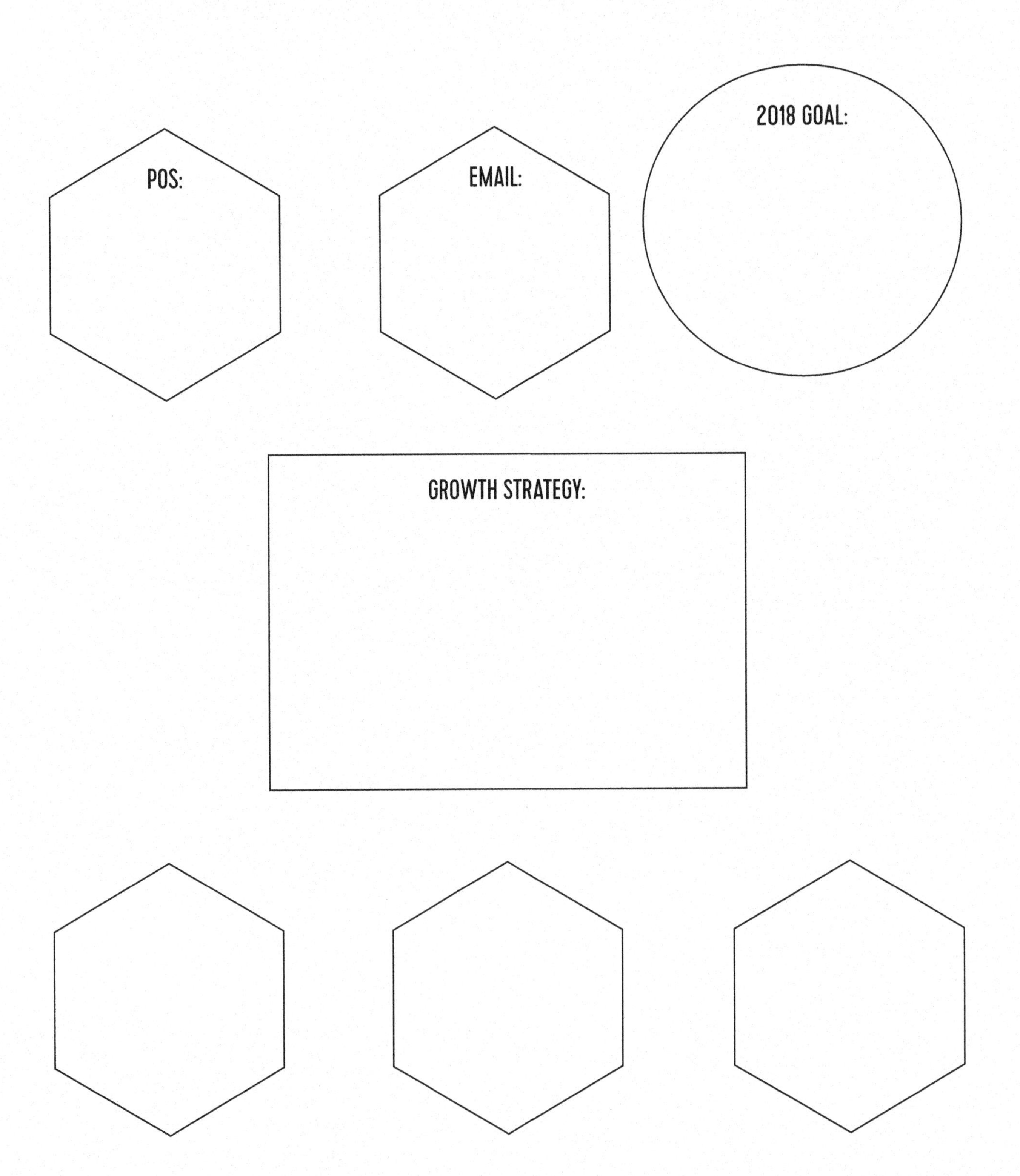

your best year

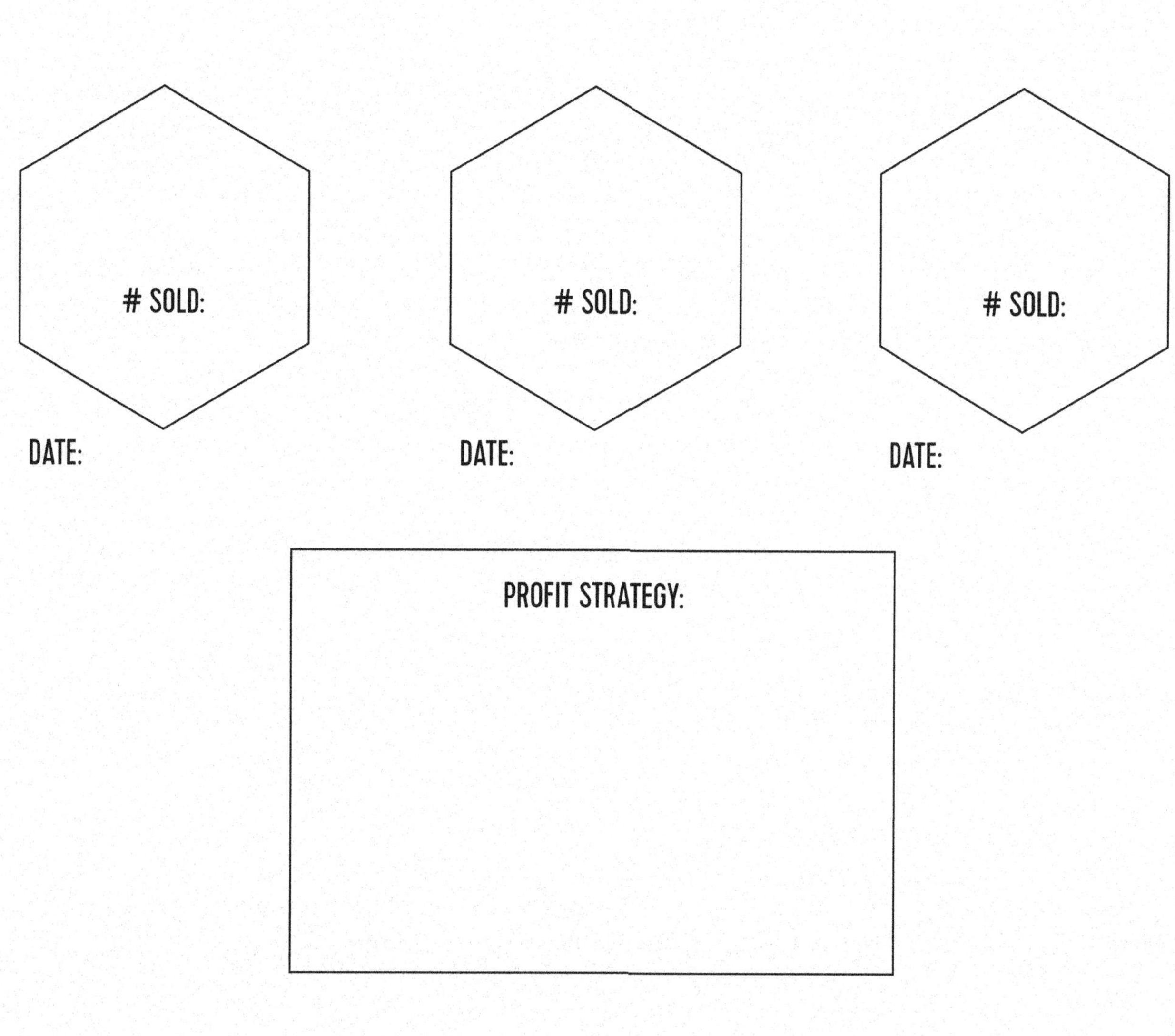

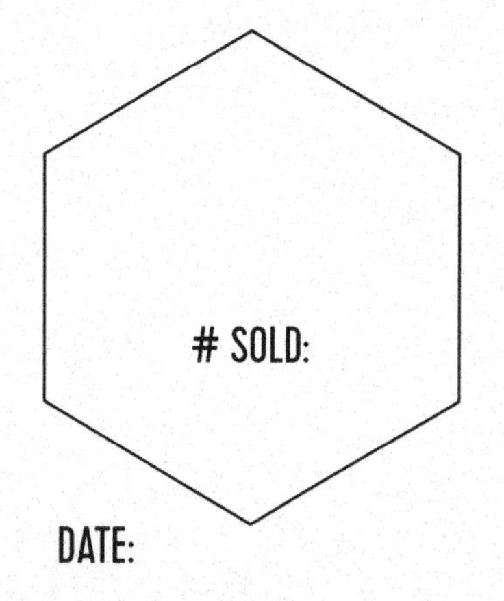

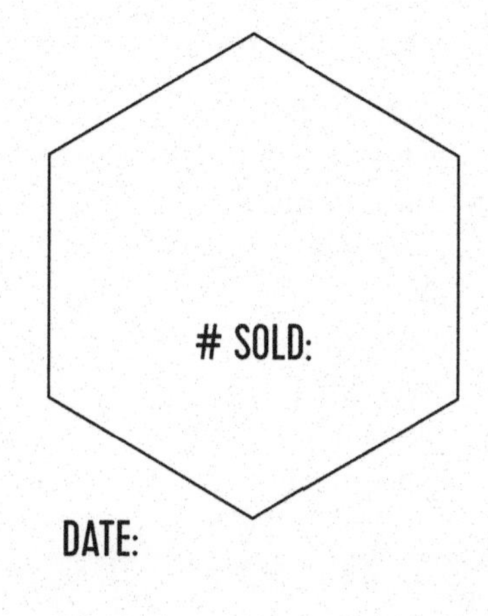

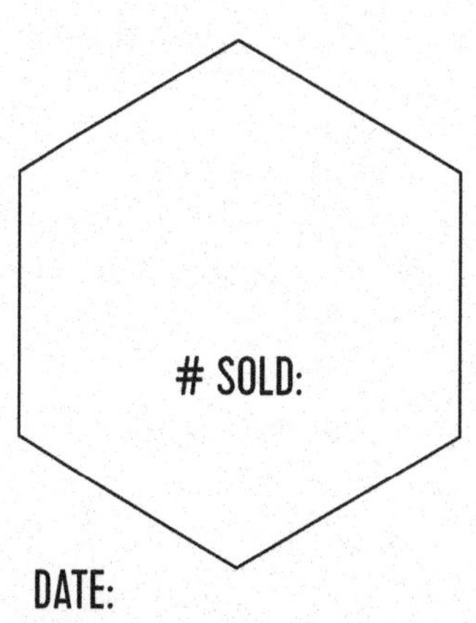

DATE:

DATE:

DATE:

The Ultimate Guide to Outsourcing

When it comes to staffing, I have a different outlook than most. As a creative business owner myself, I know it's hard to give up control on the little details that make up the work you do every day. It can also be nerve-wracking to take on the added expense. I'll show you how to hire in a way that alleviates both of those concerns.

But first, a quick disclaimer. Beware of doing for doing's sake here. As previously discussed, online business owners too often get caught up in making for making's sake, marketing for marketing's sake, emailing for emailing's sake, and training for training's sake without an end result in mind.

Do not hire for hiring's sake … don't do it because you heard you should, it seems like everyone else is, you're simply overwhelmed by a lack of schedule, or you're never sure what you should be doing next and you want to delegate some of the doing to somebody else.

If you are at all lost in logistics, or if you find yourself chasing different business advice all over the map, it is too early to hire. Save your money and the enormous chunk of time and energy it takes to feed your hire's position, and focus on your future strategy for success.

Create a customized task list. Here's how to create an extremely customized outsource list for your operation. To start, think of every task you do each week—your responsibilities in both your personal and professional life.

Next, organize all of your weekly tasks into one of three categories:

- Work that creates income
- Busywork to maintain your business
- Your household responsibilities

Then, decide which items you want to continue and which you'd like to eventually delegate. Here's a sample of my weekly tasks, organized into the three columns:

INCOME-GENERATING WORK	BUSYWORK	HOUSEHOLD CHORES
blog	*blog graphics*	*housecleaning*
books	*video production and set-up*	*ironing*
video training	*video editing*	*laundry*
marketing strategy	*video transcriptions*	*yard work*
sales	*product shipping*	*grocery shopping*
lead generation	*customer support*	*meal planning*
courses/classes	*accounting*	*cooking*
	social media management	*personal shopping*
	photography	

life and business task list

KEY:

MINE TO CONTINUE

TASK TO DELEGATE

TASK ALREADY DELEGATED

INCOME-GENERATING WORK	BUSYWORK	HOUSEHOLD CHORES

Once my responsibilities are organized into these three categories, I create a key and decide which tasks I want to continue (marked with a closed dot), which tasks I would like to delegate (marked with an open dot), and which tasks I've already delegated (marked with an x).

● MINE TO CONTINUE
○ TASK TO DELEGATE
x TASK ALREADY DELEGATED

INCOME-GENERATING WORK

● *blog*
● *books*
● *video training*
● *marketing strategy*
● *sales*
● *lead generation*
● *courses/classes*

BUSYWORK

○ *blog graphics*
x *video production and set-up*
x *video editing*
x *video transcriptions*
x *product shipping*
x *customer support*
x *accounting*
○ *social media management*
x *photography*

HOUSEHOLD CHORES

x *housecleaning*
x *ironing*
x *laundry*
x *yard work*
○ *grocery shopping*
○ *meal planning*
○ *cooking*
● *personal shopping*

Contrary to a lot of advice on hiring, I suggest you first delegate the tasks that are easiest to give up, such as the housecleaning. The hiring process for household help is simple—at most, it's an interview, a reference check, and a brief discussion about what areas need covered. It gives you a chance to communicate and manage terms of employment. And from there, you let the pros do their thing. *No training necessary.*

Training an assistant for your business is time-consuming. Even worse, you'll have to walk away from income-generating responsibilities at the very moment you take on a new expense. It's not the most comfortable transition; again, why I love the housekeepers! Let them free up a few extra hours of your time each week, and use it to work ahead and cover your absence before you hire for business.

As your business grows, so will the income you earn with every hour invested. The typical start-up mentality ("I must do everything myself!") can quickly bottleneck your business' growth, as it did mine. This means that something you create is very valuable to your customer (thereby generating a substantial income), and you are trying to do it and everything else on your business to-do list, all by yourself.

Outsourcing forces you to prioritize your task list and focus on profits and gain. We are in business, after all. It's not just about loving your work and pursuing your calling. To do more of what you love, your business has to always earn a healthy profit.

When you hire, you take on a new expense that will force you to look at your to-do list with new eyes. In online business, we often get so caught up in the day-to-day agenda that we fail to calculate projections for future growth. More often than not, you probably find yourself flying by the seat of your pants. *Even my most successful, six-figure earning clients admit to doing this!*

When I finally hired my long-term assistant and right-hand woman, Jennie, the first thing I did was sit down with the "money list" (a list of my moneymakers prioritized in order of importance and need). It was a detailed itinerary of all the things we were going to complete together in order to make my business more money this year.

This helps to create constant progress toward completion. In my early trial and errors with hiring, I've let the assistant get ahead of me on the workload. I quickly found myself racing to catch up so that I could give her more work to do, which always left me wondering, "With the way I have this set up, who's working for who?" It truly felt like I was always working to give the assistant more work!

The way it's set up now, Jennie always knows what to work on next. She follows the money list. Here are just a few things that have been completed in the last six months …

- The Summer Shift: A Private Coaching Concentrate for Inspired Entrepreneurs
- *Marketing Playbook: Scale Your Online Business to Outrageous Success*
- Private training and videos for the Luminaries Club™
- The Luminaries Club™ affiliate program (for members only)
- A three-part video training series, *Become a Best-Selling Strategist*
- *Your Best Year 2018* Launch Party and Workshop (a live event)
- *Your Best Year 2018: Productivity Workbook and Online Business Planner*

My assistant works 20 hours per week on my business, same as me. As I work on new content, Jennie has a series of daily rounds she makes for my business, and she typically takes care of these tasks first thing in the morning: ship Etsy orders, manage my various Facebook groups, and answer any customer support queries or billing issues.

I like to keep my operation lean and mean, so I've already built my system to operate, sell, and support my clients in my absence. If you're hiring to help manage all of the admin you can never get on top of, you might want to reevaluate the system, resolve the reasons so many people need to contact you, or restrict or reduce access to yourself altogether.

I liken my business to a doctor's practice. Imagine an experienced physician—studied, trained, and skilled—answering her own phones, recording new patient information, monitoring each person's blood pressure and temperature, taking her own notes and records, and doing the billing at the end of each appointment. *Would you respect her expertise more or less for it?*

How about if you had her email address and felt entitled to ask questions, send comments, and make requests on demand? Just because you're in online business does not mean you need to have an open-email policy. Professionals need to set boundaries and reserve their time and energy for paying clients.

Jennie isn't paid to handle a large amount of questions, requests, complaints, and customer issues because they're a rare occurrence. I have a system that delivers and satisfies. Instead, she spends most of her time working with me on income-generating projects from the "money list."

From the list of bulleted projects, Jennie edited *Marketing Playbook* while I built sales materials for my coaching concentrate, The Summer Shift. She attended each private one-on-one session to record action items and follow up with my clients.

Once the *Marketing Playbook* file was complete, she reformatted the entire thing for both the print and Kindle versions. In the meantime, I filmed a course for the the Luminaries Club™. We taped the course with a live audience, and in between *Marketing Playbook* formatting, Jennie moderated those webcasts.

As I started the next project (this book), Jennie edited the videos of all eight modules I just taped, designed the workbooks, and updated the course pages inside the club. By the time she finished, *Your Best Year 2018* was ready edit.

And when I don't have a current project that takes priority, Jennie is hard at work combining some of my former classes, programs, and training into the next book I'll launch. The last time I saw the project, it was over 100 pages already. It's my book, it's halfway done, and I haven't even opened the document yet! *Imagine that.*

Common Pitfalls to Avoid

Before you hire, clearly define work hours, policies, and an outline of duties expected. I also recommend adding your own "money list"—let your hire know the events or projects that you're going to roll out a year in advance.

Be crystal clear in your delivery, expectations, and requirements. With a lot of emails racing back and forth between you two, things will become open to interpretation if you don't specifically state what you want. Being indirect or indecisive is a recipe for disaster, so any communication that has been misinterpreted must be corrected promptly.

I respect Jennie's work, I genuinely like her as a person, and I've always been very upfront that this is business. There is nothing I won't approach her about, and if I find myself thinking twice about anything she's done, I open an email, tell her how I feel, and ask very direct questions.

I have to know where I stand with people, so in my opinion, the best thing I can do is always let other people know where they stand with me. It is all too easy for tension to creep into a relationship that lacks communication. There's no room for that kind of energy in my schedule!

Do not over-prepare your hire's workload. My best example of this involves my bi-weekly housecleaning crew. When they first started, the lady in charge asked me if I wanted them to change the bed sheets each week. I did, but at first I didn't have all the fresh bedding I needed to cover the change. I used to launder the sheets and immediately put them back on the beds.

It seemed such a rich luxury to have all of the bedding changed for me! So, I went out and purchased enough sets to cover all the beds, and the next time they came, I had laid out all the replacement sheets in matching piles for every bed in my household.

This is where things go awry. For every housecleaning, I had chores to do. I made sure all the sheets in the house were sorted and arranged in front of the appropriate beds. One time when I forgot, so did they (or thought I didn't want them changed because I didn't lay out the materials), and I wound up doing the work I was paying someone else to do better!

Over-preparing the work trains your hire that they need your involvement to get tasks done. We had a talk, and now my housecleaning crew finds all the clean bedding in an unsorted, badly folded pile in my towel closet each visit.

Don't delegate work daily, or even weekly. This is a huge mistake. Your hire will quickly catch up on your task list, and you will race to feed their position. As I've said, work off of a "money list" or priorities that only need reviewed occasionally.

Jennie and I are fortunate to live in the same state, so we meet quarterly to do big picture planning. We share project status updates, I tell her where I see us headed for the coming quarter, and we each walk away with a notebook full of plans.

Close your court to ball return. This one is vital for my wellbeing and sanity! I've been in professional relationships where the ball is always being hit back into my court. As in, I hire someone to do a job, explain in great detail exactly what I want, and throw them the ball. *But it keeps coming back like someone turned on the ball return machine.*

I hire for two reasons and two reasons only: (1) to earn more, and (2) to buy solutions. Habitual ball returners provide neither (without tons of hassle) and cost way more than just money. It's a passive-aggressive dance and delay on promises. It's them saying, "I don't want to work on this right now, so I'll email you a line of questions that are unnecessary to the project's progress so you'll think I'm working on this right now." Your hire's job is not to return the ball like a game of tennis, but to catch it and turn it into either more money or better solutions for your business.

A ball-returning hire is the inverse of you over-preparing the workload, but with the same end result. In the first scenario, they train you to be available when they work for you, in the second scenario, you train them to need you in order to work. Both are equally bad and incredibly frustrating. People who are hired to support you shouldn't need your constant support.

Know your seasons. Have a working marketing calendar before bringing anyone on. Hire and train before it gets busy, and aim to get the most bang for your buck.

How can every one hour of training take at least four hours off your plate each month?

When you hire, it should offer a huge return on investment and bring great relief; the only way to make it so is by doing it with a game plan for highest return and maximum efficiency.

EVERY DAY ACTION

I'm genuinely excited for you right now. You have already done more than most to reach your goals. This is where the rubber meets the road. Welcome to your action plan.

If you are going to create *everything* you want this year, you need:

- A clear survey of the land: WHERE are you and what are you up against?
- Big reasons WHY you want to build the land into something greater
- A clear vision of WHAT you're going to build
- A strategy for HOW you're going to build it
- An airtight schedule for WHEN you'll work on it
- The action plan that defines WHO you'll become to achieve it

Long Game, Short Goals

Motivation is always going to be highest when the tasks required of you feel the easiest, or your perception of effort is the lowest. Therefore, motivation is intense at the starting point of any new project or idea, as discussed in the "Entrepreneurial Stages" in *Your Best Year 2017.*[1]

Even with selfishly good reasons *why* you want to complete a project (as exercised on page 58), the intensity of motivation you experience when the project is shiny and new cannot be reproduced at later stages.

Worse, we move finish lines back by resetting our zeros. For example, I remember the days when I dreamt of having 1,000 subscribers on my email list. I visualized how successful I would feel to have that many people eager to hear about my updates and promotions. Not surprisingly, that number came and went without notice. At around 750 subscribers my sights were set on 5,000 subscribers. Before I'd even reached it, 1,000 subscribers became my new zero.

It is time to break that pattern once and for all. You are going to organize your **vision** into quarterly (three-month) **goals**, set monthly **agendas**, organize weekly **task lists**, and daily **activities**. Your plans are organized this way to keep the vision long, and the goals short.

From *How Bad Do you Want It?*, "If the goal seems to fall out of reach at any point, the [entrepreneur] is likely to back off her effort. If the goal seems attainable, but only with increased effort, the [entrepreneur] is likely to increase her effort, provided she's not already at her limit."

Create simpler lists of tasks and shorter deadlines to exploit motivational intensity in quarterly blocks. This will help you to achieve more than you currently think possible.

---

[1]http://www.marketyourcreativity.com/2017/08/entrepreneurial-stages-new-idea-next-level/

The Power of Threes

This is a simple formula that encourages you to work in threes, and more specifically: three weeks, three months, and three years. It not only helps you create a profitable year, but also encourages your career in the most authentic direction imaginable.

#1 List what you'd like to accomplish with the rest of the year you're in. For example, let's say you want to launch a new product and double last year's income.

Next ask: If I stayed on this course, where would it get me in three years? Make a projection of growth and income to ensure you like where the plan leads. Per our example, you would continue to repeat the same product launch once or twice per year.

#2 What will I have to do in the next three months to get started on this plan? This question gives birth to a progress log of tasks and to-do's. Progress logs will help you stay on track with your annual objectives, and they appear quarterly throughout the dated section of the book.

#3 What will I have to do in the next three weeks to make progress?

How to Create a Progress Log

A progress log is a method of organizing your tasks to ensure you move the needle on your annual goals. First, create a Bullet Journal™-style rapid log (aka brain dump, in which you rapidly list pending obligations, ideas, events, and tasks, in no particular order, just to get them out of your head and onto paper). Write down all you want to accomplish in the quarter ahead.

With that list, start to curate your progress log. Ask yourself:

- What special occasions or events will I honor in the next three months?
- What personal goals do I need to complete (or make progress on)?
- What nagging tasks do I need to clear up and complete?
- What new skills or techniques do I need to learn?
- What meetings or appointments need scheduled?
- What new habit do I want to start? What habit do I want to break?
- What fun dates/family time/hangouts can I schedule or plan?

Next, organize that brain dump into categories. You can use the five pillars of life: relational, spiritual, mental, physical, and financial. Or, you can use the quarterly categories I prefer: finish, do, celebrate, study, and start. (Find my example rapid log and process log on the next pages.)

On page 80, I listed a mix of personal and professional things I want to accomplish this quarter. There's no order to them, the point of the exercise is to simply release all of the things floating around in your mind that you'd like to do, change, or improve. On page 81, I categorized the rapid log into a more manageable list.

You will find your progress log worksheets every quarter (on pages 93, 121, 149, and 177).

example rapid log

- *Visit NYC to attend Money Bootcamp conference*
- *Visit Kara at Planner Con!*
- *Celebrate Jay's birthday*
- *Decorate our home for Halloween*
- *Pick the final home colors, book painters*
- *Buy a dining room set*
- *Make Become a Best-Selling Strategist an evergreen campaign*
- *Refine the work pace—get back to a schedule with margin*
- *Finish Mel Robbins' training*
- *Finish quarterly/outstanding tax paperwork*
- *Build the new launch workshop for the club*
- *Schedule launch bonus discovery calls*
- *Take the Money Bootcamp online*
- *Finish books in office + notes*
- *Launch podcast*
- *Batch podcast ahead (at least 6—8 weeks)*
- *Celebrate wrapping day!*
- *Honor downtime in December*
- *Schedule movie days and family time*
- *Get hair colored and cut*
- *Book appointment at medspa*
- *Decorate for Christmas*
- *Set up New Year for a New You review*
- *Book first 2018 vacation*
- *Final steps for Tatum's driver's license*
- *Turn 52-Week Challenge into Sunday posts*
- *Schedule social ahead on Postcron*

example progress log

FINISH

- *All open study materials (digital courses, books, and notes)*
- *Outstanding tax paperwork and bookkeeping requests*
- *Launch bonus: discovery calls*
- *Become a Best-Selling Strategist training series and campaign*
- *Your Best Year 2018 promotions*
- *Home interior: paint and dining room set*

DO

- *Launch the podcast and batch future episodes*
- *Get hair done and visit medspa*
- *Book first 2018 vacation*
- *Enjoy December! You've worked so hard for this precious downtime*
- *Decorate for the holidays*

CELEBRATE

- *Jay's birthday*
- *NYC with Kara!*
- *Halloween*
- *Thanksgiving*
- *Wrapping day*
- *Holiday movies and downtime*
- *Christmas and New Year review*

STUDY

- *Mel Robbins*
- *Money Bootcamp*
- *Books in office*
- *Facebook engagement*

START

- *52-Week Challenge to Sunday posts (2018)*
- *New Year for a New You review*
- *A more refined pace—schedule with margin*

A Schedule with Margin

Looking at your progress log, you might be left wondering: *How will I get all this done?* That's normal! I have the answer for you right here.

Have you seen the exercise floating around about creating an ideal day? The gist is, you list everything you would do on an ideal day, from the time you wake up until the time you go to bed. The idea is to create the perfect daily schedule, and that exercise agitates me to my core!

I don't want one ideal day. The average American only gets 29,200 days in their lifetime; I want each of mine to be gloriously enriching and unique! So, I cringe at the idea of scheduling one day from start to finish and calling it ideal.

What I do love is an ideal weekly schedule, in which you outline an optimal workweek. That way, you can get your work done and then *go live* your enriching and glorious life around it! After all, my motto is …

your life, your business, your way

I want you to create a routine for project completion, and set the pace for a marathon, not a sprint. Try not to charge full speed ahead, but rather methodically apply effort in such a way that the work keeps you always eager to get back to it.

For example, the excitement of a new product might tempt you to skip meals and put in extra hours under extreme, self-imposed deadlines. Trust me, that's a recipe for disaster.

Instead, give yourself a comfortable timeline and set hours you can maintain for the duration. There are two guarantees on this roller coaster ride to the next level: Projects will always take longer than you think and the muddy stages will always be thicker than you imagined.

"A SCHEDULE DEFENDS FROM CHAOS AND WHIM. IT IS A NET FOR CATCHING DAYS."—Annie Dillard

Stephen Covey's "big rocks" method (which he learned during another business expert's lecture) is my favorite way to organize a schedule. Here's the story, in his own words:

> "As this man stood in front of the group of high-powered over-achievers he said, 'Okay, time for a quiz.' Then he pulled out a one-gallon, wide-mouthed mason jar and set it on a table in front of him. Then he produced about a dozen fist-sized rocks and carefully placed them, one at a time, into the jar.
>
> When the jar was filled to the top and no more rocks would fit inside, he asked, 'Is this jar full?' Everyone in the class said, 'Yes.' Then he said, 'Really?' He reached under the table and pulled out a bucket of gravel. Then he dumped some gravel in and shook the

> jar causing pieces of gravel to work themselves down into the spaces between the big rocks.
>
> Then he smiled and asked the group once more, 'Is the jar full?' By this time, the class was onto him. 'Probably not,' one of them answered. 'Good!' he replied. And he reached under the table and brought out a bucket of sand. He started dumping the sand in and it went into all the spaces left between the rocks and the gravel. Once more he asked the question, 'Is this jar full?'
>
> 'No!' the class shouted. Once again he said, 'Good!' Then he grabbed a pitcher of water and began to pour it in until the jar was filled to the brim. Then he looked up at the class and asked, 'What is the point of this illustration?'
>
> One eager beaver raised his hand and said, 'The point is, no matter how full your schedule is, if you try really hard, you can always fit some more things into it!'
>
> 'No,' the speaker replied, 'that's not the point. The truth this illustration teaches us is: If you don't put the big rocks in first, you'll never get them in at all.'
>
> What are the big rocks in your life? A project that you want to accomplish? Time with your loved ones? Your faith, your education, your finances? A cause? Teaching or mentoring others? [Put them] in first or you'll never get them in at all."

Your schedule can and should be custom-fit to your lifestyle. Some people make magic with the "eat that frog" method — which means, they wake up and do the most daunting task on their list, and then finish whatever else needs doing. Others work in distraction-free time chunks, as we've discussed. And still others take note of their most productive hours of the day, and maximize them by applying laser-focused effort during that period.

As you will see in my example schedule on page 87, I combine all of these techniques. I use the "big rock" method by working backwards from my annual vision. Each day, I put the big rocks first during my first two powerblocks of the morning (my most productive time).

We all have to complete tasks that overwhelm or otherwise burden us. Leave no stone unturned until you find the system that works best for you.

Add Margin

Listen, my friends: the internet is not that interesting. It is not changing nearly as much as you click to see if it's changed. I can guarantee you that checking your email and Instagram account 80 times a day is not going to get you your goals. It is a bad habit of mindlessly seeking validation and safety in an endless and unfulfilling loop.

Wouldn't life be so much better if instead you had meaningful white space in your day? Imagine having time to learn a new hobby, take up a sport with a loved one, or indulgently get lost in a favorite fiction for hours—completely uninterrupted.

My theory? Luxurious white space is 100% available to us if we'd cut out nagging energy drains, unfinished business, emotional vampires, useless busywork, mindless clicking, and otherwise stop wasting hours on things that don't matter.

On my plan, you allot time for everything that needs to get done while leaving margin (or extra padding) in and between those tasks.

A week scheduled too strictly creates constant pressure. People who exist in a state of constant pressure tend to get stuck in their head. Being stuck in your head leads to unnecessary worry thought, which triggers survival mechanisms, which results in panic. It is a vicious cycle, a self-induced pressure cooker.

As we learned in survival, when people are panicked, they have no idea what they're doing or WHY, so they rely on outworn patterns and old routines. They create more of the same mess.

"[WORKING] IN A STATE OF PRESSURE-INDUCED SELF-CONSCIOUSNESS IS LIKE FIRE WALKING WHILE GIVING YOUR FULL ATTENTION TO THE PAINFUL HEAT IN YOUR FEET RATHER THAN FOCUSING ON WHERE YOU'RE GOING."—Matt Fitzgerald

One thing that is often missing from our schedules is a healthy dose of white space. You are creative, as we all are, and you need time to dream, strategize, and explore new opportunities every week (if not every day).

An ideal schedule is going to include a lot of focus with plenty of room to *breathe*. Have you been breathing lately? The feast-or-famine pressure-cooker we often create for ourselves doesn't allow many healthy deep breaths! It's time to remedy that once and for all.

Some essentials for your ideal work week are tasks that keeps you on time, tasks that gets you ahead, tasks that allow you to seek and find new customers for your business, time to clear up unfinished business, and breaks that allow you to refuel your creative energy on a regular basis.

If you find this exercise to be challenging—because there's too much to fit in—something's not right. Remember, busyness is a form of laziness. Either you don't have the right systems in place, you're doing too much work that doesn't matter (and seeing little growth and profit from it), or you're doing everything yourself, making good money, and bottlenecking your business by not outsourcing. If you can't create a schedule with margin, something is fundamentally off.

Who Do You Need to Become?

In the book *Compound Effect*, Darren Hardy introduced goal-setting in a way that was brand new to me. Typically, we set a goal and then say, "Okay, what do I have to do to get it?" He says, "The question we should be asking ourselves is: 'Who do I need to become?'"

This was a game-changer for me, and it hit home right away. Hardy quotes Jim Rohn as teaching, "If you want to have more, you have to become more. Success is not something you pursue. What you pursue will elude you; it can be like trying to chase butterflies. Success is something you attract by the person you become."

WHO MUST YOU BECOME TO ATTRACT WHAT YOU WANT?

Whether it is a new relationship, a healthier body, a better income, dream clients—whatever the goal—this question can be applied. If it's the perfect spouse, what kind of person would he be attracted to? Who would *you* have to become in order to attract your ideal partner? What qualities and characteristics do you need to enhance to be a perfect match?

If it's a dozen dream clients, what kind of professional would they be attracted to? Who do *you* have to become to attract them? What skills and abilities do you need to sharpen in order to be a worthy hire to that crowd?

If it's a higher salary, what kind of person would the money be attracted to? Who do *you* have to become to attract it? What habits, routines, and ethics do you need to improve in order to produce the high quality work it requires?

Online entrepreneurs have a tendency to "make do" with their operation while waiting for it to make larger amounts of money, so that they can afford to stop making do with their operation!

Last year, I realized that if I want to earn upwards of 100K, I needed a 100K plan combined with a 100K mindset. I needed to make 100K decisions. It required a 100K work ethic. And most of all, I needed to believe my business was worth every single dollar! I had to think and behave like that successful business owner in order to become her.

I don't have to ask, I know you're excited about these new concepts! Let's go map it out.

a schedule with margin

WHAT TASKS CANNOT BE SCHEDULED IN ADVANCE? WHAT MUST YOU DO IN REAL-TIME EACH WEEK? WHEN AND HOW OFTEN MUST YOU DO THESE TASKS?

WHAT WORK COULD YOU SCHEDULE IN ADVANCE THAT WILL HELP YOU GET AHEAD EACH WEEK?

WHEN WILL YOU BATCH AND COMPLETE TASKS THAT MAY HELP CREATE NEW LEADS FOR YOUR BUSINESS?

WHEN WILL YOU COMPLETE ADMINISTRATIVE TASKS, UNFINISHED BUSINESS, AND PROFESSIONAL SELF-CARE?

ARRANGE THESE TASKS INTO YOUR TYPICAL WORKING DAYS OF THE WEEK.

example answers

WHAT TASKS CANNOT BE SCHEDULED IN ADVANCE? WHAT MUST YOU DO IN REAL-TIME EACH WEEK? WHEN AND HOW OFTEN MUST YOU DO THESE TASKS?

- *Club conversations, live calls, and updates—3x week*
- *Time-sensitive blog posts (i.e. monthly income report)—monthly*
- *Customer support and sales questions—3x week*

WHAT WORK COULD YOU SCHEDULE IN ADVANCE THAT WILL HELP YOU GET AHEAD EACH WEEK?

- *Blog posts*
- *Sales emails*
- *Social media posts and conversation starters*
- *Workshops and masterclasses*

WHEN WILL YOU BATCH AND COMPLETE TASKS THAT MAY HELP CREATE NEW LEADS FOR YOUR BUSINESS?

Thursdays are a great day to reserve for this. I'll work on ...
- *lead generation,*
- *product development, and*
- *repurposing content for new audiences and outlets.*

WHEN WILL YOU COMPLETE ADMINISTRATIVE TASKS, UNFINISHED BUSINESS, AND PROFESSIONAL SELF-CARE?

Wednesdays and Fridays can be dedicated to wrapping up any unfinished business and de-cluttering my inbox. I'd also love to cut out of work early and hit the gym on these days.

In the chart below, *bullets represent 90-minute powerblocks.*

ARRANGE THESE TASKS INTO YOUR TYPICAL WORKING DAYS OF THE WEEK.

Monday	*Tuesday*	*Wednesday*	*Thursday*	*Friday*
• *New product production (this block always generates income)* • *Blog post* • *Blog post*	• *New product production* • *Blog post* • *Schedule weekly email, finish blog posts*	• *New product production* • *New product production* *Cut out early and go to the gym.*	• *New product production* • *New lead generation* • *New lead generation*	• *New product production* • *Admin and social updates* *Cut out early and go to the gym.*

who must you become?

WHAT ARE THE DISCREPANCIES BETWEEN WHAT YOU WANT AND THE ACTIONS YOU TAKE?

WHAT ACTIONS DO YOU KNOW YOU NEED TO TAKE IN ORDER TO ACHIEVE YOUR ANNUAL VISION?

WHO DO YOU NEED TO BECOME TO ENSURE THESE ACTIONS ARE TAKEN?

IN ORDER TO BECOME THIS VERSION OF YOURSELF, WHAT ARE SOME BAD HABITS AND COMFORTS YOU MUST GIVE UP? IN OTHER WORDS, WHAT SHOULD YOU STOP DOING? WHAT WILL YOU DO INSTEAD?

example answers

WHAT ARE THE DISCREPANCIES BETWEEN WHAT YOU WANT AND THE ACTIONS YOU TAKE?

I wait too long to start projects (I spend weeks researching and mapping things out) and then end up smashed against the deadline—or—I add things at the last minute, and I'm not prepared far enough ahead to handle the extra workload.

WHAT ACTIONS DO YOU KNOW YOU NEED TO TAKE IN ORDER TO ACHIEVE YOUR ANNUAL VISION?

I can achieve my annual vision, and how I arrive—calm and collected, or disheveled and exhausted—is entirely up to me. I need to stop planning to work ahead and start actually doing it!

I need to get ahead of my schedule and work ahead on my editorial calendar.

WHO DO YOU NEED TO BECOME TO ENSURE THESE ACTIONS ARE TAKEN?

I need to become the kind of person who accepts the process of creation as part of the job. I need to stop resisting the hard parts and tackle obstacles as soon as they arise.

IN ORDER TO BECOME THIS VERSION OF YOURSELF, WHAT ARE SOME BAD HABITS AND COMFORTS YOU MUST GIVE UP? IN OTHER WORDS, WHAT SHOULD YOU STOP DOING? WHAT WILL YOU DO INSTEAD?

Stop clicking the internet >>> Start shutting down the laptop after work at 3PM
Stop incessantly checking email >>> Start adding it to the schedule, allowing time to respond
Stop social media looping >>> Start checking in at the end of the day, in only one touch
Stop evening device time >>> Start reading fiction
Stop hesitating, shrinking, and hiding >>> Become camera- and opportunity-ready!

Open, Closed, and New Business

Each month, you will be prompted to list open, closed, and new business, an idea I developed after attending neighborhood board meetings. At the end of each meeting, board members reviewed open (outstanding) issues, closed (completed) issues, and new issues to tackle.

When I first implemented this practice into my routine, my list of open business went on for days. It was unnerving! As mentioned, completion is the key to success.

This is one of my favorite additions to this year's routine as it brings awareness to the number of new ideas you chase at any given time. Find it on the first page of every monthly review.

Track Your Abundance

If you're anything like I was, you probably check your email all day, literally waiting for sales to appear. Because I checked and deleted all day, I never really knew how much I earned. Then I read the book, *Get Rich, Lucky Bitch!* by Denise Duffield-Thomas and everything changed. Her idea to track and record abundance was one of my favorite takeaways, and I've adapted this into a worksheet for your monthly review.

Here's the gist: Money flows into your life every day, and unless you record it, you really have no idea how wealthy you are or how healthy your business is. Each month, I write a financial goal that challenges me, and then think of a reward for achieving it. I have shattered income ceilings using this method, rewarding myself things, such as a bi-weekly housecleaning crew, a Disney Cruse for my family, a private sitting room sanctuary for myself, and a spontaneous trip to San Francisco—all paid in full.

I visit my abundance tracker every morning and record the previous day's income before deleting payment notifications and completed orders. At the top of the worksheet, I write a few things I'm trying to accomplish that month (e.g. "Offset a project-building month, attract interested clients"). At the bottom, I list some ways to achieve my goal (e.g. "course launch, book clearance, membership dues"). I also use that space below to list financial goals I'll complete by meeting this income (e.g. "Car paid, savings goal met, salary in reserve").

I hope this exercise becomes as profitable for you as it has been for me. You will find it on the fourth page each month.

Daily Scorecard and Weekly Review

The final thing I have to unveil in this year's routine is the weekly review and daily scorecard. In order to help you make the most of every week, I've added some tough questions that have helped shaped my year in a very positive way.

I then added a scoring system to the review: each circle represents 25%, and you're aiming to give 100% as often as possible! Use this to score your commitment, focus, and follow-through throughout the week. Find these exercises on the fifth and sixth pages each month.

your annual objectives

SUMMARIZED FROM PAGE 46

FINANCIAL:

SPIRITUAL:

MENTAL:

PHYSICAL:

RELATIONAL:

my annual goals

quarter one rapid log

-
-
-
-
-
-
-
-
-
-
-
-
-
-
-
-
-
-
-
-
-
-
-
-
-
-
-

quarter one progress log

FINISH

DO

CELEBRATE

STUDY

START

january

TASKS & TO-DO LIST	SUNDAY	MONDAY	TUESDAY
OPEN		1	2
	7	8	9
CLOSED	14	15	16
NEW	21	22	23
	28	29	30

2018

WEDNESDAY	THURSDAY	FRIDAY	SATURDAY
3	4	5	6
10	11	12	13
17	18	19	20
24	25	26	27
31			

january focus

FINANCIAL:

SPIRITUAL:

MENTAL:

PHYSICAL:

RELATIONAL:

tasks to complete

WEEK OF THE 1ST	WEEK OF THE 8TH	WEEK OF THE 15TH	WEEK OF THE 22ND	WEEK OF THE 29TH

january income

MONTHLY CHALLENGE:

EARN ____________ IN JANUARY!

TO ACCOMPLISH THIS MONTH:

01/01	WEEK ONE	01/14	01/20	01/26
01/02	01/08	WEEK TWO	01/21	01/27
01/03	01/09	01/15	WEEK THREE	01/28
01/04	01/10	01/16	01/22	WEEK FOUR
01/05	01/11	01/17	01/23	01/29
01/06	01/12	01/18	01/24	01/30
01/07	01/13	01/19	01/25	01/31

TOTAL EARNED:

REWARD:

IDEAS TO HELP MEET THIS CHALLENGE:

weekly review

QUESTIONS	JANUARY 1–7	JANUARY 8–14
WHAT DID I ACHIEVE THIS WEEK?		
WHAT HELPED ME TO ACHIEVE THESE THINGS?		
WHAT HINDERED MY PRODUCTIVITY?		
WHAT WILL I CHANGE NEXT WEEK?		

january

JANUARY 15–21

JANUARY 22–28

DAILY SCORECARD

M
T
W
T
F
S
S

M
T
W
T
F
S
S

M
T
W
T
F
S
S

M
T
W
T
F
S
S

january review

GROWTH TRACKER — RECORD YOUR END-MONTH NUMBERS, FANS, AND FOLLOWERS.

FB	PINTEREST	EMAIL	VIEWS	SALES	[ ]	[ ]	[ ]	[ ]
____	____	____	____	____	____	____	____	____

circle the metrics you will work to improve next month

GOAL TRACKER — RECORD YOUR PROGRESS AND CHALLENGES THIS MONTH.

FINANCIAL:

SPIRITUAL:

MENTAL:

PHYSICAL:

RELATIONAL:

MOST IMPORTANT TO ME RIGHT NOW?

DOES MY SCHEDULE NEED REARRANGEMENT?

PROFIT TRACKER — RECORD THIS MONTH'S INCOME, SALARY, AND EXPENSES.

TOTAL EARNED (YEAR-TO-DATE):

january review

PROJECTS COMPLETED THIS MONTH

WHAT WORKED WELL THIS MONTH?

PROJECTS STILL IN THE WORKS

HOW CAN I MULTIPLY THESE RESULTS?

WHAT OBSTACLE(S) AM I FACING?

WHY IS IT DIFFICULT?

HOW HAVE I TRIED TO OVERCOME IT?

WHAT CAN I TRY NEXT?

DID THIS MONTH GET ME CLOSER TO MY ANNUAL OBJECTIVES?

IF YES, HOW WILL I KEEP UP THE MOMENTUM?

IF NO, WHAT WILL I DO TO GET BACK ON TRACK?

february

TASKS & TO-DO LIST	SUNDAY	MONDAY	TUESDAY
OPEN			
	4	5	6
CLOSED	11	12	13
NEW	18	19	20
	25	26	27

2018

WEDNESDAY	THURSDAY	FRIDAY	SATURDAY
	1	2	3
7	8	9	10
14	15	16	17
21	22	23	24
28			

february focus

FINANCIAL:

SPIRITUAL:

MENTAL:

PHYSICAL:

RELATIONAL:

tasks to complete

WEEK OF THE 29TH	WEEK OF THE 5TH	WEEK OF THE 12TH	WEEK OF THE 19TH	WEEK OF THE 25TH

february income

MONTHLY CHALLENGE:

TO ACCOMPLISH THIS MONTH:

EARN IN FEBRUARY!

02/01	WEEK ONE	02/14	02/20	02/26
02/02	02/08	WEEK TWO	02/21	02/27
02/03	02/09	02/15	WEEK THREE	02/28
02/04	02/10	02/16	02/22	WEEK FOUR
02/05	02/11	02/17	02/23	
02/06	02/12	02/18	02/24	
02/07	02/13	02/19	02/25	

TOTAL EARNED:

REWARD:

IDEAS TO HELP MEET THIS CHALLENGE:

weekly review

QUESTIONS	JAN 29—FEB 4	FEBRUARY 5—11
WHAT DID I ACHIEVE THIS WEEK?		
WHAT HELPED ME TO ACHIEVE THESE THINGS?		
WHAT HINDERED MY PRODUCTIVITY?		
WHAT WILL I CHANGE NEXT WEEK?		

february

FEBRUARY 12–18

FEBRUARY 19–25

DAILY SCORECARD

M	○	○	○	○
T	○	○	○	○
W	○	○	○	○
T	○	○	○	○
F	○	○	○	○
S	○	○	○	○
S	○	○	○	○
M	○	○	○	○
T	○	○	○	○
W	○	○	○	○
T	○	○	○	○
F	○	○	○	○
S	○	○	○	○
S	○	○	○	○
M	○	○	○	○
T	○	○	○	○
W	○	○	○	○
T	○	○	○	○
F	○	○	○	○
S	○	○	○	○
S	○	○	○	○
M	○	○	○	○
T	○	○	○	○
W	○	○	○	○
T	○	○	○	○
F	○	○	○	○
S	○	○	○	○
S	○	○	○	○

february review

GROWTH TRACKER – RECORD YOUR END-MONTH NUMBERS, FANS, AND FOLLOWERS.

FB PINTEREST EMAIL VIEWS SALES [ ] [ ] [ ] [ ]

circle the metrics you will work to improve next month

GOAL TRACKER – RECORD YOUR PROGRESS AND CHALLENGES THIS MONTH.

FINANCIAL:

SPIRITUAL:

MENTAL:

PHYSICAL:

RELATIONAL:

MOST IMPORTANT TO ME RIGHT NOW?

DOES MY SCHEDULE NEED REARRANGEMENT?

PROFIT TRACKER – RECORD THIS MONTH'S INCOME, SALARY, AND EXPENSES.

TOTAL EARNED (YEAR-TO-DATE):

february review

PROJECTS COMPLETED THIS MONTH

WHAT WORKED WELL THIS MONTH?

HOW CAN I MULTIPLY THESE RESULTS?

PROJECTS STILL IN THE WORKS

WHAT OBSTACLE(S) AM I FACING?

WHY IS IT DIFFICULT?

HOW HAVE I TRIED TO OVERCOME IT?

WHAT CAN I TRY NEXT?

DID THIS MONTH GET ME CLOSER TO MY ANNUAL OBJECTIVES?

IF YES, HOW WILL I KEEP UP THE MOMENTUM?

IF NO, WHAT WILL I DO TO GET BACK ON TRACK?

march

TASKS & TO-DO LIST	SUNDAY	MONDAY	TUESDAY
OPEN			
	4	5	6
CLOSED	11	12	13
NEW	18	19	20
	25	26	27

2018

WEDNESDAY	THURSDAY	FRIDAY	SATURDAY
	1	2	3
7	8	9	10
14	15	16	17
21	22	23	24
28	29	30	31

march focus

FINANCIAL:

SPIRITUAL:

MENTAL:

PHYSICAL:

RELATIONAL:

tasks to complete

WEEK OF THE 26TH	WEEK OF THE 5TH	WEEK OF THE 12TH	WEEK OF THE 19TH	WEEK OF THE 26TH

march income

MONTHLY CHALLENGE:

TO ACCOMPLISH THIS MONTH:

EARN ______ IN MARCH!

03/01	WEEK ONE	03/14	03/20	03/26
03/02	03/08	WEEK TWO	03/21	03/27
03/03	03/09	03/15	WEEK THREE	03/28
03/04	03/10	03/16	03/22	WEEK FOUR
03/05	03/11	03/17	03/23	03/29
03/06	03/12	03/18	03/24	03/30
03/07	03/13	03/19	03/25	03/31

TOTAL EARNED:

REWARD:

IDEAS TO HELP MEET THIS CHALLENGE:

weekly review

QUESTIONS	FEB 26—MAR 4	MARCH 5—11
WHAT DID I ACHIEVE THIS WEEK?		
WHAT HELPED ME TO ACHIEVE THESE THINGS?		
WHAT HINDERED MY PRODUCTIVITY?		
WHAT WILL I CHANGE NEXT WEEK?		

march

MARCH 12–18

MARCH 19–25

DAILY SCORECARD

M	○	○	○	○
T	○	○	○	○
W	○	○	○	○
T	○	○	○	○
F	○	○	○	○
S	○	○	○	○
S	○	○	○	○
M	○	○	○	○
T	○	○	○	○
W	○	○	○	○
T	○	○	○	○
F	○	○	○	○
S	○	○	○	○
S	○	○	○	○
M	○	○	○	○
T	○	○	○	○
W	○	○	○	○
T	○	○	○	○
F	○	○	○	○
S	○	○	○	○
S	○	○	○	○
M	○	○	○	○
T	○	○	○	○
W	○	○	○	○
T	○	○	○	○
F	○	○	○	○
S	○	○	○	○
S	○	○	○	○

march review

GROWTH TRACKER – RECORD YOUR END-MONTH NUMBERS, FANS, AND FOLLOWERS.

FB	PINTEREST	EMAIL	VIEWS	SALES	[ ]	[ ]	[ ]	[ ]
____	____	____	____	____	____	____	____	____

circle the metrics you will work to improve next month

GOAL TRACKER – RECORD YOUR PROGRESS AND CHALLENGES THIS MONTH.

FINANCIAL:

SPIRITUAL:

MENTAL:

PHYSICAL:

RELATIONAL:

MOST IMPORTANT TO ME RIGHT NOW?

DOES MY SCHEDULE NEED REARRANGEMENT?

PROFIT TRACKER – RECORD THIS MONTH'S INCOME, SALARY, AND EXPENSES.

TOTAL EARNED (YEAR-TO-DATE):

march review

PROJECTS COMPLETED THIS MONTH

PROJECTS STILL IN THE WORKS

DID THIS MONTH GET ME CLOSER TO MY ANNUAL OBJECTIVES?

IF YES, HOW WILL I KEEP UP THE MOMENTUM?

IF NO, WHAT WILL I DO TO GET BACK ON TRACK?

WHAT WORKED WELL THIS MONTH?

HOW CAN I MULTIPLY THESE RESULTS?

WHAT OBSTACLE(S) AM I FACING?

WHY IS IT DIFFICULT?

HOW HAVE I TRIED TO OVERCOME IT?

WHAT CAN I TRY NEXT?

YOUR ANNUAL STRATEGY

APRIL	MAY	JUNE	JULY

AUGUST	SEPTEMBER	OCTOBER	NOVEMBER

DECEMBER	JANUARY	FEBRUARY	MARCH

your annual objectives

REVISE AND UPDATE FROM PAGE 91

FINANCIAL:

SPIRITUAL:

MENTAL:

PHYSICAL:

RELATIONAL:

my annual goals

quarter two rapid log

•
•
•
•
•
•
•
•
•
•
•
•
•
•
•
•
•
•
•
•
•
•
•
•
•
•

quarter two progress log

FINISH

DO

CELEBRATE

STUDY

START

april

TASKS & TO-DO LIST	SUNDAY	MONDAY	TUESDAY
OPEN	1	2	3
	8	9	10
CLOSED	15	16	17
NEW	22	23	24
	29	30	

2018

WEDNESDAY	THURSDAY	FRIDAY	SATURDAY
4	5	6	7
11	12	13	14
18	19	20	21
25	26	27	28

april focus

FINANCIAL:

SPIRITUAL:

MENTAL:

PHYSICAL:

RELATIONAL:

tasks to complete

WEEK OF THE 2ND	WEEK OF THE 9TH	WEEK OF THE 16TH	WEEK OF THE 23RD	WEEK OF THE 30TH

april income

MONTHLY CHALLENGE:

TO ACCOMPLISH THIS MONTH:

EARN ____________ IN APRIL!

04/01	WEEK ONE	04/14	04/20	04/26
04/02	04/08	WEEK TWO	04/21	04/27
04/03	04/09	04/15	WEEK THREE	04/28
04/04	04/10	04/16	04/22	WEEK FOUR
04/05	04/11	04/17	04/23	04/29
04/06	04/12	04/18	04/24	04/30
04/07	04/13	04/19	04/25	

TOTAL EARNED:

REWARD:

IDEAS TO HELP MEET THIS CHALLENGE:

weekly review

QUESTIONS	APRIL 2–8	APRIL 9–15
WHAT DID I ACHIEVE THIS WEEK?		
WHAT HELPED ME TO ACHIEVE THESE THINGS?		
WHAT HINDERED MY PRODUCTIVITY?		
WHAT WILL I CHANGE NEXT WEEK?		

april

APRIL 16—22

APRIL 23—29

DAILY SCORECARD

M
T
W
T
F
S
S

M
T
W
T
F
S
S

M
T
W
T
F
S
S

M
T
W
T
F
S
S

april review

GROWTH TRACKER – RECORD YOUR END-MONTH NUMBERS, FANS, AND FOLLOWERS.

FB	PINTEREST	EMAIL	VIEWS	SALES	[ ]	[ ]	[ ]	[ ]
____	____	____	____	____	____	____	____	____

circle the metrics you will work to improve next month

GOAL TRACKER – RECORD YOUR PROGRESS AND CHALLENGES THIS MONTH.

FINANCIAL:

SPIRITUAL:

MENTAL:

PHYSICAL:

RELATIONAL:

MOST IMPORTANT TO ME RIGHT NOW?

DOES MY SCHEDULE NEED REARRANGEMENT?

PROFIT TRACKER – RECORD THIS MONTH'S INCOME, SALARY, AND EXPENSES.

TOTAL EARNED (YEAR-TO-DATE):

april review

PROJECTS COMPLETED THIS MONTH

WHAT WORKED WELL THIS MONTH?

HOW CAN I MULTIPLY THESE RESULTS?

PROJECTS STILL IN THE WORKS

WHAT OBSTACLE[S] AM I FACING?

WHY IS IT DIFFICULT?

HOW HAVE I TRIED TO OVERCOME IT?

WHAT CAN I TRY NEXT?

DID THIS MONTH GET ME CLOSER TO MY ANNUAL OBJECTIVES?

IF YES, HOW WILL I KEEP UP THE MOMENTUM?

IF NO, WHAT WILL I DO TO GET BACK ON TRACK?

may

TASKS & TO-DO LIST	SUNDAY	MONDAY	TUESDAY
OPEN			1
	6	7	8
CLOSED	13	14	15
NEW	20	21	22
	27	28	29

2018

WEDNESDAY	THURSDAY	FRIDAY	SATURDAY
2	3	4	5
9	10	11	12
16	17	18	19
23	24	25	26
30	31		

may focus

FINANCIAL:

SPIRITUAL:

MENTAL:

PHYSICAL:

RELATIONAL:

tasks to complete

WEEK OF THE 30TH	WEEK OF THE 7TH	WEEK OF THE 14TH	WEEK OF THE 21ST	WEEK OF THE 28TH

may income

MONTHLY CHALLENGE:

EARN IN MAY!

TO ACCOMPLISH THIS MONTH:

05/01	WEEK ONE	05/14	05/20	05/26
05/02	05/08	WEEK TWO	05/21	05/27
05/03	05/09	05/15	WEEK THREE	05/28
05/04	05/10	05/16	05/22	WEEK FOUR
05/05	05/11	05/17	05/23	05/29
05/06	05/12	05/18	05/24	05/30
05/07	05/13	05/19	05/25	05/31

TOTAL EARNED:

REWARD:

IDEAS TO HELP MEET THIS CHALLENGE:

weekly review

QUESTIONS	APR 30—MAY 6	MAY 7—13
WHAT DID I ACHIEVE THIS WEEK?		
WHAT HELPED ME TO ACHIEVE THESE THINGS?		
WHAT HINDERED MY PRODUCTIVITY?		
WHAT WILL I CHANGE NEXT WEEK?		

may

MAY 14–20	MAY 21–27	DAILY SCORECARD

M ○ ○ ○ ○
T ○ ○ ○ ○
W ○ ○ ○ ○
T ○ ○ ○ ○
F ○ ○ ○ ○
S ○ ○ ○ ○
S ○ ○ ○ ○

M ○ ○ ○ ○
T ○ ○ ○ ○
W ○ ○ ○ ○
T ○ ○ ○ ○
F ○ ○ ○ ○
S ○ ○ ○ ○
S ○ ○ ○ ○

M ○ ○ ○ ○
T ○ ○ ○ ○
W ○ ○ ○ ○
T ○ ○ ○ ○
F ○ ○ ○ ○
S ○ ○ ○ ○
S ○ ○ ○ ○

M ○ ○ ○ ○
T ○ ○ ○ ○
W ○ ○ ○ ○
T ○ ○ ○ ○
F ○ ○ ○ ○
S ○ ○ ○ ○
S ○ ○ ○ ○

may review

GROWTH TRACKER – RECORD YOUR END-MONTH NUMBERS, FANS, AND FOLLOWERS.

FB	PINTEREST	EMAIL	VIEWS	SALES	[ ]	[ ]	[ ]	[ ]

circle the metrics you will work to improve next month

GOAL TRACKER – RECORD YOUR PROGRESS AND CHALLENGES THIS MONTH.

FINANCIAL:

SPIRITUAL:

MENTAL:

PHYSICAL:

RELATIONAL:

MOST IMPORTANT TO ME RIGHT NOW?

DOES MY SCHEDULE NEED REARRANGEMENT?

PROFIT TRACKER – RECORD THIS MONTH'S INCOME, SALARY, AND EXPENSES.

TOTAL EARNED (YEAR-TO-DATE):

may review

PROJECTS COMPLETED THIS MONTH

PROJECTS STILL IN THE WORKS

DID THIS MONTH GET ME CLOSER TO MY ANNUAL OBJECTIVES?

IF YES, HOW WILL I KEEP UP THE MOMENTUM?

IF NO, WHAT WILL I DO TO GET BACK ON TRACK?

WHAT WORKED WELL THIS MONTH?

HOW CAN I MULTIPLY THESE RESULTS?

WHAT OBSTACLE(S) AM I FACING?

WHY IS IT DIFFICULT?

HOW HAVE I TRIED TO OVERCOME IT?

WHAT CAN I TRY NEXT?

june

TASKS & TO-DO LIST	SUNDAY	MONDAY	TUESDAY
OPEN			
	3	4	5
CLOSED	10	11	12
NEW	17	18	19
	24	25	26

2018

WEDNESDAY	THURSDAY	FRIDAY	SATURDAY
		1	2
6	7	8	9
13	14	15	16
20	21	22	23
27	28	29	30

june focus

FINANCIAL:

SPIRITUAL:

MENTAL:

PHYSICAL:

RELATIONAL:

tasks to complete

WEEK OF THE 28TH	WEEK OF THE 4TH	WEEK OF THE 11TH	WEEK OF THE 18TH	WEEK OF THE 25TH

june income

MONTHLY CHALLENGE:

TO ACCOMPLISH THIS MONTH:

EARN ____________ IN JUNE!

06/01	WEEK ONE	06/14	06/20	06/26
06/02	06/08	WEEK TWO	06/21	06/27
06/03	06/09	06/15	WEEK THREE	06/28
06/04	06/10	06/16	06/22	WEEK FOUR
06/05	06/11	06/17	06/23	06/29
06/06	06/12	06/18	06/24	06/30
06/07	06/13	06/19	06/25	

TOTAL EARNED:

REWARD:

IDEAS TO HELP MEET THIS CHALLENGE:

weekly review

QUESTIONS	JUNE 4—10	JUNE 11—17
WHAT DID I ACHIEVE THIS WEEK?		
WHAT HELPED ME TO ACHIEVE THESE THINGS?		
WHAT HINDERED MY PRODUCTIVITY?		
WHAT WILL I CHANGE NEXT WEEK?		

june

JUNE 18—24	JUNE 25—JUL 1

DAILY SCORECARD

M	○	○	○	○
T	○	○	○	○
W	○	○	○	○
T	○	○	○	○
F	○	○	○	○
S	○	○	○	○
S	○	○	○	○
M	○	○	○	○
T	○	○	○	○
W	○	○	○	○
T	○	○	○	○
F	○	○	○	○
S	○	○	○	○
S	○	○	○	○
M	○	○	○	○
T	○	○	○	○
W	○	○	○	○
T	○	○	○	○
F	○	○	○	○
S	○	○	○	○
S	○	○	○	○
M	○	○	○	○
T	○	○	○	○
W	○	○	○	○
T	○	○	○	○
F	○	○	○	○
S	○	○	○	○
S	○	○	○	○

june review

GROWTH TRACKER – RECORD YOUR END-MONTH NUMBERS, FANS, AND FOLLOWERS.

FB PINTEREST EMAIL VIEWS SALES [ ] [ ] [ ] [ ]

circle the metrics you will work to improve next month

GOAL TRACKER – RECORD YOUR PROGRESS AND CHALLENGES THIS MONTH.

FINANCIAL:

SPIRITUAL:

MENTAL:

PHYSICAL:

RELATIONAL:

MOST IMPORTANT TO ME RIGHT NOW?

DOES MY SCHEDULE NEED REARRANGEMENT?

PROFIT TRACKER – RECORD THIS MONTH'S INCOME, SALARY, AND EXPENSES.

TOTAL EARNED (YEAR-TO-DATE):

june review

PROJECTS COMPLETED THIS MONTH

WHAT WORKED WELL THIS MONTH?

PROJECTS STILL IN THE WORKS

HOW CAN I MULTIPLY THESE RESULTS?

DID THIS MONTH GET ME CLOSER TO MY ANNUAL OBJECTIVES?

IF YES, HOW WILL I KEEP UP THE MOMENTUM?

IF NO, WHAT WILL I DO TO GET BACK ON TRACK?

WHAT OBSTACLE(S) AM I FACING?

WHY IS IT DIFFICULT?

HOW HAVE I TRIED TO OVERCOME IT?

WHAT CAN I TRY NEXT?

YOUR ANNUAL STRATEGY

JULY	AUGUST	SEPTEMBER	OCTOBER

NOVEMBER	DECEMBER	JANUARY	FEBRUARY

MARCH	APRIL	MAY	JUNE

your annual objectives

REVISE AND UPDATE FROM PAGE 119

FINANCIAL:

SPIRITUAL:

MENTAL:

PHYSICAL:

RELATIONAL:

my annual goals

quarter three rapid log

-
-
-
-
-
-
-
-
-
-
-
-
-
-
-
-
-
-
-
-
-
-
-
-
-
-
-
-

quarter three progress log

FINISH

DO

CELEBRATE

STUDY

START

july

TASKS & TO-DO LIST	SUNDAY	MONDAY	TUESDAY
OPEN	1	2	3
	8	9	10
CLOSED	15	16	17
NEW	22	23	24
	29	30	31

2018

WEDNESDAY	THURSDAY	FRIDAY	SATURDAY
4	5	6	7
11	12	13	14
18	19	20	21
25	26	27	28

july focus

FINANCIAL:

SPIRITUAL:

MENTAL:

PHYSICAL:

RELATIONAL:

tasks to complete

WEEK OF THE 2ND	WEEK OF THE 9TH	WEEK OF THE 16TH	WEEK OF THE 23RD	WEEK OF THE 30TH

july income

MONTHLY CHALLENGE:

TO ACCOMPLISH THIS MONTH:

EARN IN JULY!

07/01	WEEK ONE	07/14	07/20	07/26
07/02	07/08	WEEK TWO	07/21	07/27
07/03	07/09	07/15	WEEK THREE	07/28
07/04	07/10	07/16	07/22	WEEK FOUR
07/05	07/11	07/17	07/23	07/29
07/06	07/12	07/18	07/24	07/30
07/07	07/13	07/19	07/25	07/31

TOTAL EARNED:

REWARD:

IDEAS TO HELP MEET THIS CHALLENGE:

weekly review

QUESTIONS	JULY 2–8	JULY 9–15
WHAT DID I ACHIEVE THIS WEEK?		
WHAT HELPED ME TO ACHIEVE THESE THINGS?		
WHAT HINDERED MY PRODUCTIVITY?		
WHAT WILL I CHANGE NEXT WEEK?		

july

JULY 16—22	JULY 23—29	DAILY SCORECARD
		M ○ ○ ○ ○ T ○ ○ ○ ○ W ○ ○ ○ ○ T ○ ○ ○ ○ F ○ ○ ○ ○ S ○ ○ ○ ○ S ○ ○ ○ ○
		M ○ ○ ○ ○ T ○ ○ ○ ○ W ○ ○ ○ ○ T ○ ○ ○ ○ F ○ ○ ○ ○ S ○ ○ ○ ○ S ○ ○ ○ ○
		M ○ ○ ○ ○ T ○ ○ ○ ○ W ○ ○ ○ ○ T ○ ○ ○ ○ F ○ ○ ○ ○ S ○ ○ ○ ○ S ○ ○ ○ ○
		M ○ ○ ○ ○ T ○ ○ ○ ○ W ○ ○ ○ ○ T ○ ○ ○ ○ F ○ ○ ○ ○ S ○ ○ ○ ○ S ○ ○ ○ ○

july review

GROWTH TRACKER – RECORD YOUR END-MONTH NUMBERS, FANS, AND FOLLOWERS.

FB	PINTEREST	EMAIL	VIEWS	SALES	[ ]	[ ]	[ ]	[ ]
______	______	______	______	______	______	______	______	______

circle the metrics you will work to improve next month

GOAL TRACKER – RECORD YOUR PROGRESS AND CHALLENGES THIS MONTH.

FINANCIAL:

SPIRITUAL:

MENTAL:

PHYSICAL:

RELATIONAL:

MOST IMPORTANT TO ME RIGHT NOW?

DOES MY SCHEDULE NEED REARRANGEMENT?

PROFIT TRACKER – RECORD THIS MONTH'S INCOME, SALARY, AND EXPENSES.

TOTAL EARNED (YEAR-TO-DATE):

july review

PROJECTS COMPLETED THIS MONTH

WHAT WORKED WELL THIS MONTH?

PROJECTS STILL IN THE WORKS

HOW CAN I MULTIPLY THESE RESULTS?

DID THIS MONTH GET ME CLOSER TO MY ANNUAL OBJECTIVES?

IF YES, HOW WILL I KEEP UP THE MOMENTUM?

IF NO, WHAT WILL I DO TO GET BACK ON TRACK?

WHAT OBSTACLE(S) AM I FACING?

WHY IS IT DIFFICULT?

HOW HAVE I TRIED TO OVERCOME IT?

WHAT CAN I TRY NEXT?

august

TASKS & TO-DO LIST	SUNDAY	MONDAY	TUESDAY
OPEN			
	5	6	7
CLOSED	12	13	14
NEW	19	20	21
	26	27	28

2018

WEDNESDAY	THURSDAY	FRIDAY	SATURDAY
1	2	3	4
8	9	10	11
15	16	17	18
22	23	24	25
29	30	31	

august focus

FINANCIAL:

SPIRITUAL:

MENTAL:

PHYSICAL:

RELATIONAL:

tasks to complete

WEEK OF THE 30TH	WEEK OF THE 6TH	WEEK OF THE 13TH	WEEK OF THE 20TH	WEEK OF THE 27TH

august income

MONTHLY CHALLENGE:

TO ACCOMPLISH THIS MONTH:

EARN ______________ IN AUGUST!

08/01	WEEK ONE	08/14	08/20	08/26
08/02	08/08	WEEK TWO	08/21	08/27
08/03	08/09	08/15	WEEK THREE	08/28
08/04	08/10	08/16	08/22	WEEK FOUR
08/05	08/11	08/17	08/23	08/29
08/06	08/12	08/18	08/24	08/30
08/07	08/13	08/19	08/25	08/31

TOTAL EARNED:

REWARD:

IDEAS TO HELP MEET THIS CHALLENGE:

weekly review

QUESTIONS	JUL 30—AUG 5	AUGUST 6—12
WHAT DID I ACHIEVE THIS WEEK?		
WHAT HELPED ME TO ACHIEVE THESE THINGS?		
WHAT HINDERED MY PRODUCTIVITY?		
WHAT WILL I CHANGE NEXT WEEK?		

august

AUGUST 13–19	AUGUST 20–26

DAILY SCORECARD

M ○ ○ ○ ○
T ○ ○ ○ ○
W ○ ○ ○ ○
T ○ ○ ○ ○
F ○ ○ ○ ○
S ○ ○ ○ ○
S ○ ○ ○ ○

M ○ ○ ○ ○
T ○ ○ ○ ○
W ○ ○ ○ ○
T ○ ○ ○ ○
F ○ ○ ○ ○
S ○ ○ ○ ○
S ○ ○ ○ ○

M ○ ○ ○ ○
T ○ ○ ○ ○
W ○ ○ ○ ○
T ○ ○ ○ ○
F ○ ○ ○ ○
S ○ ○ ○ ○
S ○ ○ ○ ○

M ○ ○ ○ ○
T ○ ○ ○ ○
W ○ ○ ○ ○
T ○ ○ ○ ○
F ○ ○ ○ ○
S ○ ○ ○ ○
S ○ ○ ○ ○

august review

GROWTH TRACKER – RECORD YOUR END-MONTH NUMBERS, FANS, AND FOLLOWERS.

FB	PINTEREST	EMAIL	VIEWS	SALES	[ ]	[ ]	[ ]	[ ]
____	____	____	____	____	____	____	____	____

circle the metrics you will work to improve next month

GOAL TRACKER – RECORD YOUR PROGRESS AND CHALLENGES THIS MONTH.

FINANCIAL:

SPIRITUAL:

MENTAL:

PHYSICAL:

RELATIONAL:

MOST IMPORTANT TO ME RIGHT NOW?

DOES MY SCHEDULE NEED REARRANGEMENT?

PROFIT TRACKER – RECORD THIS MONTH'S INCOME, SALARY, AND EXPENSES.

TOTAL EARNED (YEAR-TO-DATE):

august review

PROJECTS COMPLETED THIS MONTH

PROJECTS STILL IN THE WORKS

DID THIS MONTH GET ME CLOSER TO MY ANNUAL OBJECTIVES?

IF YES, HOW WILL I KEEP UP THE MOMENTUM?

IF NO, WHAT WILL I DO TO GET BACK ON TRACK?

WHAT WORKED WELL THIS MONTH?

HOW CAN I MULTIPLY THESE RESULTS?

WHAT OBSTACLE(S) AM I FACING?

WHY IS IT DIFFICULT?

HOW HAVE I TRIED TO OVERCOME IT?

WHAT CAN I TRY NEXT?

september

TASKS & TO-DO LIST	SUNDAY	MONDAY	TUESDAY
OPEN			
	2	3	4
CLOSED	9	10	11
NEW	16	17	18
	23 / 30	24	25

2018

WEDNESDAY	THURSDAY	FRIDAY	SATURDAY
			1
5	6	7	8
12	13	14	15
19	20	21	22
26	27	28	29

september focus

FINANCIAL:

SPIRITUAL:

MENTAL:

PHYSICAL:

RELATIONAL:

tasks to complete

WEEK OF THE 27TH	WEEK OF THE 3RD	WEEK OF THE 10TH	WEEK OF THE 17TH	WEEK OF THE 24TH

september income

MONTHLY CHALLENGE:

TO ACCOMPLISH THIS MONTH:

EARN IN SEPTEMBER!

09/01	WEEK ONE	09/14	09/20	09/26
09/02	09/08	WEEK TWO	09/21	09/27
09/03	09/09	09/15	WEEK THREE	09/28
09/04	09/10	09/16	09/22	WEEK FOUR
09/05	09/11	09/17	09/23	09/29
09/06	09/12	09/18	09/24	09/30
09/07	09/13	09/19	09/25	

TOTAL EARNED:

REWARD:

IDEAS TO HELP MEET THIS CHALLENGE:

weekly review

QUESTIONS	SEPTEMBER 3–9	SEPTEMBER 10–16
WHAT DID I ACHIEVE THIS WEEK?		
WHAT HELPED ME TO ACHEIVE THESE THINGS?		
WHAT HINDERED MY PRODUCTIVITY?		
WHAT WILL I CHANGE NEXT WEEK?		

september

SEPTEMBER 17—23	SEPTEMBER 24—30	DAILY SCORECARD
		M ○ ○ ○ ○ T ○ ○ ○ ○ W ○ ○ ○ ○ T ○ ○ ○ ○ F ○ ○ ○ ○ S ○ ○ ○ ○ S ○ ○ ○ ○
		M ○ ○ ○ ○ T ○ ○ ○ ○ W ○ ○ ○ ○ T ○ ○ ○ ○ F ○ ○ ○ ○ S ○ ○ ○ ○ S ○ ○ ○ ○
		M ○ ○ ○ ○ T ○ ○ ○ ○ W ○ ○ ○ ○ T ○ ○ ○ ○ F ○ ○ ○ ○ S ○ ○ ○ ○ S ○ ○ ○ ○
		M ○ ○ ○ ○ T ○ ○ ○ ○ W ○ ○ ○ ○ T ○ ○ ○ ○ F ○ ○ ○ ○ S ○ ○ ○ ○ S ○ ○ ○ ○

september review

GROWTH TRACKER — RECORD YOUR END-MONTH NUMBERS, FANS, AND FOLLOWERS.

FB	PINTEREST	EMAIL	VIEWS	SALES	[ ]	[ ]	[ ]	[ ]
____	____	____	____	____	____	____	____	____

circle the metrics you will work to improve next month

GOAL TRACKER — RECORD YOUR PROGRESS AND CHALLENGES THIS MONTH.

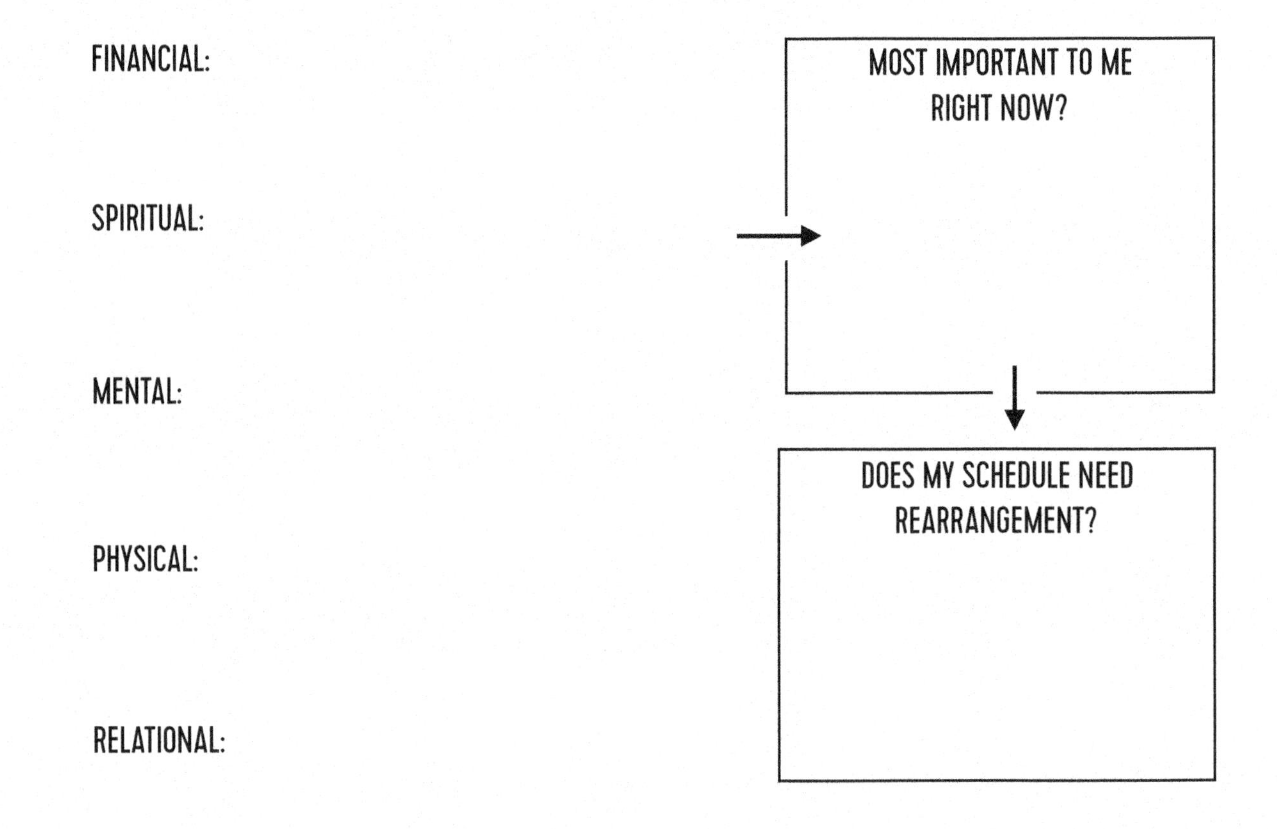

FINANCIAL:

SPIRITUAL:

MENTAL:

PHYSICAL:

RELATIONAL:

MOST IMPORTANT TO ME RIGHT NOW?

DOES MY SCHEDULE NEED REARRANGEMENT?

PROFIT TRACKER — RECORD THIS MONTH'S INCOME, SALARY, AND EXPENSES.

TOTAL EARNED (YEAR-TO-DATE):

september review

PROJECTS COMPLETED THIS MONTH

WHAT WORKED WELL THIS MONTH?

HOW CAN I MULTIPLY THESE RESULTS?

PROJECTS STILL IN THE WORKS

WHAT OBSTACLE(S) AM I FACING?

WHY IS IT DIFFICULT?

HOW HAVE I TRIED TO OVERCOME IT?

WHAT CAN I TRY NEXT?

DID THIS MONTH GET ME CLOSER TO MY ANNUAL OBJECTIVES?

IF YES, HOW WILL I KEEP UP THE MOMENTUM?

IF NO, WHAT WILL I DO TO GET BACK ON TRACK?

YOUR ANNUAL STRATEGY

OCTOBER	NOVEMBER	DECEMBER	JANUARY

FEBRUARY	MARCH	APRIL	MAY

JUNE	JULY	AUGUST	SEPTEMBER

your annual objectives

REVISE AND UPDATE FROM PAGE 147

FINANCIAL:

SPIRITUAL:

MENTAL:

PHYSICAL:

RELATIONAL:

my annual goals

quarter four rapid log

-
-
-
-
-
-
-
-
-
-
-
-
-
-
-
-
-
-
-
-
-
-
-
-
-
-
-

quarter four progress log

FINISH

DO

CELEBRATE

STUDY

START

october

TASKS & TO-DO LIST	SUNDAY	MONDAY	TUESDAY
OPEN		1	2
	7	8	9
CLOSED	14	15	16
NEW	21	22	23
	28	29	30

2018

WEDNESDAY	THURSDAY	FRIDAY	SATURDAY
3	4	5	6
10	11	12	13
17	18	19	20
24	25	26	27
31			

october focus

FINANCIAL:

SPIRITUAL:

MENTAL:

PHYSICAL:

RELATIONAL:

tasks to complete

WEEK OF THE 1ST	WEEK OF THE 8TH	WEEK OF THE 15TH	WEEK OF THE 22ND	WEEK OF THE 29TH

october income

MONTHLY CHALLENGE:

TO ACCOMPLISH THIS MONTH:

EARN IN OCTOBER!

10/01	WEEK ONE	10/14	10/20	10/26
10/02	10/08	WEEK TWO	10/21	10/27
10/03	10/09	10/15	WEEK THREE	10/28
10/04	10/10	10/16	10/22	WEEK FOUR
10/05	10/11	10/17	10/23	10/29
10/06	10/12	10/18	10/24	10/30
10/07	10/13	10/19	10/25	10/31

TOTAL EARNED:

REWARD:

IDEAS TO HELP MEET THIS CHALLENGE:

weekly review

QUESTIONS	OCTOBER 1–7	OCTOBER 8–14
WHAT DID I ACHIEVE THIS WEEK?		
WHAT HELPED ME TO ACHIEVE THESE THINGS?		
WHAT HINDERED MY PRODUCTIVITY?		
WHAT WILL I CHANGE NEXT WEEK?		

october

OCTOBER 15–21	OCTOBER 22–28	DAILY SCORECARD
		M ○ ○ ○ ○ T ○ ○ ○ ○ W ○ ○ ○ ○ T ○ ○ ○ ○ F ○ ○ ○ ○ S ○ ○ ○ ○ S ○ ○ ○ ○
		M ○ ○ ○ ○ T ○ ○ ○ ○ W ○ ○ ○ ○ T ○ ○ ○ ○ F ○ ○ ○ ○ S ○ ○ ○ ○ S ○ ○ ○ ○
		M ○ ○ ○ ○ T ○ ○ ○ ○ W ○ ○ ○ ○ T ○ ○ ○ ○ F ○ ○ ○ ○ S ○ ○ ○ ○ S ○ ○ ○ ○
		M ○ ○ ○ ○ T ○ ○ ○ ○ W ○ ○ ○ ○ T ○ ○ ○ ○ F ○ ○ ○ ○ S ○ ○ ○ ○ S ○ ○ ○ ○

october review

GROWTH TRACKER – RECORD YOUR END-MONTH NUMBERS, FANS, AND FOLLOWERS.

FB	PINTEREST	EMAIL	VIEWS	SALES	[ ]	[ ]	[ ]	[ ]
____	____	____	____	____	____	____	____	____

circle the metrics you will work to improve next month

GOAL TRACKER – RECORD YOUR PROGRESS AND CHALLENGES THIS MONTH.

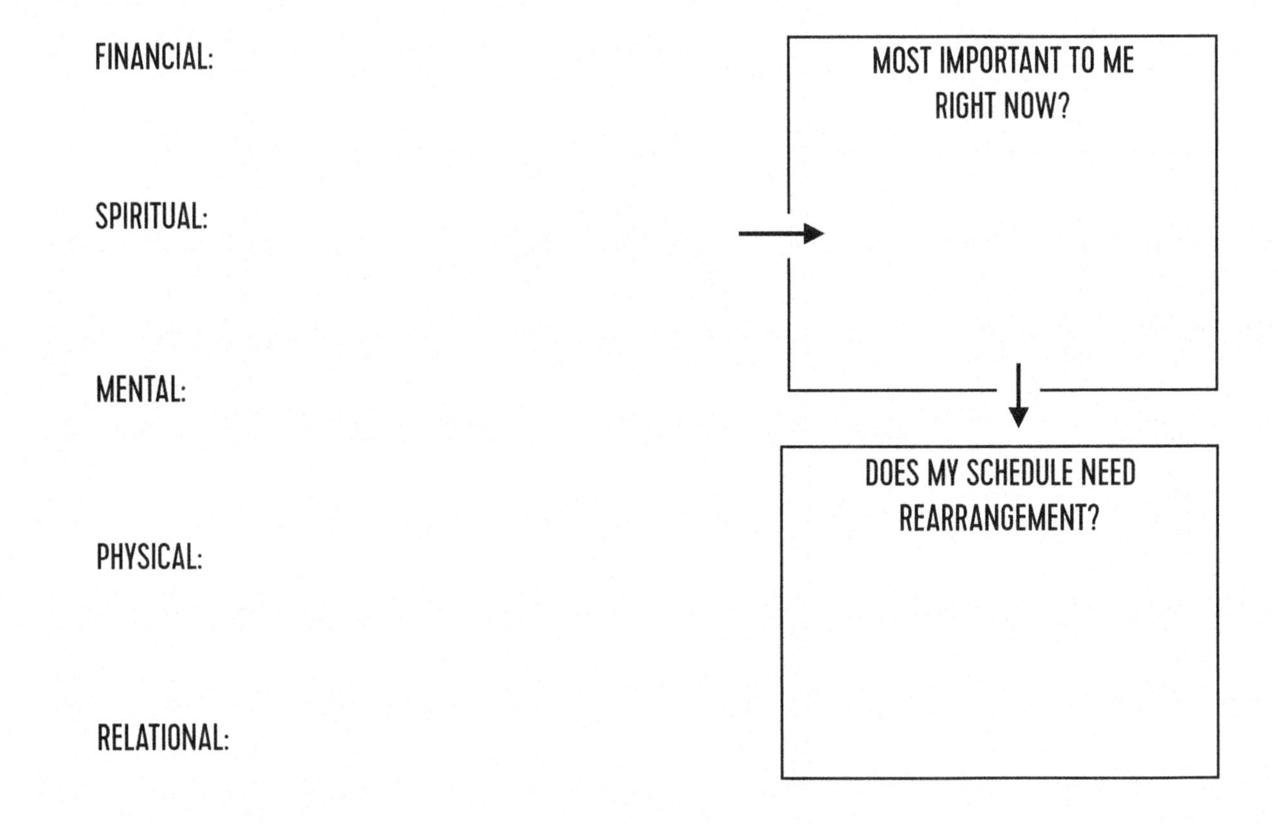

FINANCIAL:

SPIRITUAL:

MENTAL:

PHYSICAL:

RELATIONAL:

MOST IMPORTANT TO ME RIGHT NOW?

DOES MY SCHEDULE NEED REARRANGEMENT?

PROFIT TRACKER – RECORD THIS MONTH'S INCOME, SALARY, AND EXPENSES.

TOTAL EARNED (YEAR-TO-DATE):

october review

PROJECTS COMPLETED THIS MONTH

WHAT WORKED WELL THIS MONTH?

HOW CAN I MULTIPLY THESE RESULTS?

PROJECTS STILL IN THE WORKS

WHAT OBSTACLE(S) AM I FACING?

WHY IS IT DIFFICULT?

HOW HAVE I TRIED TO OVERCOME IT?

WHAT CAN I TRY NEXT?

DID THIS MONTH GET ME CLOSER TO MY ANNUAL OBJECTIVES?

IF YES, HOW WILL I KEEP UP THE MOMENTUM?

IF NO, WHAT WILL I DO TO GET BACK ON TRACK?

november

TASKS & TO-DO LIST	SUNDAY	MONDAY	TUESDAY
OPEN			
	4	5	6
CLOSED	11	12	13
NEW	18	19	20
	25	26	27

2018

WEDNESDAY	THURSDAY	FRIDAY	SATURDAY
	1	2	3
7	8	9	10
14	15	16	17
21	22	23	24
28	29	30	

november focus

FINANCIAL:

SPIRITUAL:

MENTAL:

PHYSICAL:

RELATIONAL:

tasks to complete

WEEK OF THE 29TH	WEEK OF THE 5TH	WEEK OF THE 12TH	WEEK OF THE 19TH	WEEK OF THE 26TH

november income

MONTHLY CHALLENGE:

TO ACCOMPLISH THIS MONTH:

EARN IN NOVEMBER!

11/01	WEEK ONE	11/14	11/20	11/26
11/02	11/08	WEEK TWO	11/21	11/27
11/03	11/09	11/15	WEEK THREE	11/28
11/04	11/10	11/16	11/22	WEEK FOUR
11/05	11/11	11/17	11/23	11/29
11/06	11/12	11/18	11/24	11/30
11/07	11/13	11/19	11/25	

TOTAL EARNED:

REWARD:

IDEAS TO HELP MEET THIS CHALLENGE:

weekly review

QUESTIONS	OCT 29—NOV 4	NOVEMBER 5—11
WHAT DID I ACHIEVE THIS WEEK?		
WHAT HELPED ME TO ACHIEVE THESE THINGS?		
WHAT HINDERED MY PRODUCTIVITY?		
WHAT WILL I CHANGE NEXT WEEK?		

november

NOVEMBER 12—18	NOVEMBER 19—25	DAILY SCORECARD
		M ○ ○ ○ ○ T ○ ○ ○ ○ W ○ ○ ○ ○ T ○ ○ ○ ○ F ○ ○ ○ ○ S ○ ○ ○ ○ S ○ ○ ○ ○
		M ○ ○ ○ ○ T ○ ○ ○ ○ W ○ ○ ○ ○ T ○ ○ ○ ○ F ○ ○ ○ ○ S ○ ○ ○ ○ S ○ ○ ○ ○
		M ○ ○ ○ ○ T ○ ○ ○ ○ W ○ ○ ○ ○ T ○ ○ ○ ○ F ○ ○ ○ ○ S ○ ○ ○ ○ S ○ ○ ○ ○
		M ○ ○ ○ ○ T ○ ○ ○ ○ W ○ ○ ○ ○ T ○ ○ ○ ○ F ○ ○ ○ ○ S ○ ○ ○ ○ S ○ ○ ○ ○

november review

GROWTH TRACKER – RECORD YOUR END-MONTH NUMBERS, FANS, AND FOLLOWERS.

FB	PINTEREST	EMAIL	VIEWS	SALES	[ ]	[ ]	[ ]	[ ]
______	______	______	______	______	______	______	______	______

circle the metrics you will work to improve next month

GOAL TRACKER – RECORD YOUR PROGRESS AND CHALLENGES THIS MONTH.

FINANCIAL:

SPIRITUAL:

MENTAL:

PHYSICAL:

RELATIONAL:

MOST IMPORTANT TO ME RIGHT NOW?

DOES MY SCHEDULE NEED REARRANGEMENT?

PROFIT TRACKER – RECORD THIS MONTH'S INCOME, SALARY, AND EXPENSES.

TOTAL EARNED (YEAR-TO-DATE):

november review

PROJECTS COMPLETED THIS MONTH

WHAT WORKED WELL THIS MONTH?

HOW CAN I MULTIPLY THESE RESULTS?

PROJECTS STILL IN THE WORKS

WHAT OBSTACLE(S) AM I FACING?

WHY IS IT DIFFICULT?

HOW HAVE I TRIED TO OVERCOME IT?

WHAT CAN I TRY NEXT?

DID THIS MONTH GET ME CLOSER TO MY ANNUAL OBJECTIVES?

IF YES, HOW WILL I KEEP UP THE MOMENTUM?

IF NO, WHAT WILL I DO TO GET BACK ON TRACK?

december

TASKS & TO-DO LIST	SUNDAY	MONDAY	TUESDAY
OPEN			
	2	3	4
CLOSED	9	10	11
NEW	16	17	18
	23 / 30	24 / 31	25

2018

WEDNESDAY	THURSDAY	FRIDAY	SATURDAY
			1
5	6	7	8
12	13	14	15
19	20	21	22
26	27	28	29

december focus

FINANCIAL:

SPIRITUAL:

MENTAL:

PHYSICAL:

RELATIONAL:

tasks to complete

WEEK OF THE 3RD	WEEK OF THE 10TH	WEEK OF THE 17TH	WEEK OF THE 24TH	WEEK OF THE 31ST

december income

MONTHLY CHALLENGE:

TO ACCOMPLISH THIS MONTH:

EARN IN DECEMBER!

12/01	WEEK ONE	12/14	12/20	12/26
12/02	12/08	WEEK TWO	12/21	12/27
12/03	12/09	12/15	WEEK THREE	12/28
12/04	12/10	12/16	12/22	WEEK FOUR
12/05	12/11	12/17	12/23	12/29
12/06	12/12	12/18	12/24	12/30
12/07	12/13	12/19	12/25	12/31

TOTAL EARNED:

REWARD:

IDEAS TO HELP MEET THIS CHALLENGE:

weekly review

QUESTIONS	NOV 26–DEC 2	DECEMBER 3–9
WHAT DID I ACHIEVE THIS WEEK?		
WHAT HELPED ME TO ACHIEVE THESE THINGS?		
WHAT HINDERED MY PRODUCTIVITY?		
WHAT WILL I CHANGE NEXT WEEK?		

december

DECEMBER 10–16	DECEMBER 17–23

DAILY SCORECARD

M ○ ○ ○ ○
T ○ ○ ○ ○
W ○ ○ ○ ○
T ○ ○ ○ ○
F ○ ○ ○ ○
S ○ ○ ○ ○
S ○ ○ ○ ○

M ○ ○ ○ ○
T ○ ○ ○ ○
W ○ ○ ○ ○
T ○ ○ ○ ○
F ○ ○ ○ ○
S ○ ○ ○ ○
S ○ ○ ○ ○

M ○ ○ ○ ○
T ○ ○ ○ ○
W ○ ○ ○ ○
T ○ ○ ○ ○
F ○ ○ ○ ○
S ○ ○ ○ ○
S ○ ○ ○ ○

M ○ ○ ○ ○
T ○ ○ ○ ○
W ○ ○ ○ ○
T ○ ○ ○ ○
F ○ ○ ○ ○
S ○ ○ ○ ○
S ○ ○ ○ ○

december review

GROWTH TRACKER – RECORD YOUR END-MONTH NUMBERS, FANS, AND FOLLOWERS.

FB	PINTEREST	EMAIL	VIEWS	SALES	[ ]	[ ]	[ ]	[ ]
____	____	____	____	____	____	____	____	____

circle the metrics you will work to improve next month

GOAL TRACKER – RECORD YOUR PROGRESS AND CHALLENGES THIS MONTH.

FINANCIAL:

SPIRITUAL:

MENTAL:

PHYSICAL:

RELATIONAL:

MOST IMPORTANT TO ME RIGHT NOW?

DOES MY SCHEDULE NEED REARRANGEMENT?

PROFIT TRACKER – RECORD THIS MONTH'S INCOME, SALARY, AND EXPENSES.

TOTAL EARNED (YEAR-TO-DATE):

december review

PROJECTS COMPLETED THIS MONTH

WHAT WORKED WELL THIS MONTH?

HOW CAN I MULTIPLY THESE RESULTS?

PROJECTS STILL IN THE WORKS

WHAT OBSTACLE(S) AM I FACING?

WHY IS IT DIFFICULT?

HOW HAVE I TRIED TO OVERCOME IT?

WHAT CAN I TRY NEXT?

DID THIS MONTH GET ME CLOSER TO MY ANNUAL OBJECTIVES?

IF YES, HOW WILL I KEEP UP THE MOMENTUM?

IF NO, WHAT WILL I DO TO GET BACK ON TRACK?

BEWARE THE DARK SIDE

The slow seasons in business can become ruts of pure disgruntlement. You'll know you are here when things feel …

- restless and tense all at once;
- like nothing's going your way;
- stalled and stuck, and the last thing you want to do is work;
- drained from putting into a business that's not giving back; and
- suddenly anti-social (sharing your work becomes a chore).

If you can relate, I'll bet you're in online business! A slump is an unproductive cacophony of "I should's" and "f–k its." It feels miserable, and how you feel about your business is never a good measure of its success.

This isn't about what happened last month or what online campaign didn't produce the results that you anticipated yesterday. It is about understanding the peaks and crests of your business so that you can plan and persist accordingly.

During slow periods, it is natural to consume more than you create. For us that means more clicking, comparing, and checking; we're all prone to the same weaknesses. Grant Cardone, author of *The 10X Rule,* describes this as being used by social media rather than using it—such an important distinction.

Slumps like these produce enormous amounts of tension in and around the lull, which is why it feels miserable. The only thing that cures the rut is probably the last thing you want to do, which is to take action.

This summer, when my income dipped and business slowed, I too landed in a slump zone. To get myself out of that disgruntled state, I had to face the thing I was avoiding. There was a project ahead of me. It's one that I love with all of my heart, but it also consumes my life and promises great periods of grind. Which brings me to my point …

To beat a slump in business, you must physically move out of it.

Constant and consistent movement is paramount to your success. The underlying movement of marketing is the best part of business. It is a dance, and it can be perfectly choreographed to create maximum enjoyment for all.

But if you are not already dancing, customers can't join in. You're always the lead partner. If the cause of your rut isn't a slow season (which is quite natural for all businesses), the 30-90 Rule is your next line of questioning.

 THE 30-90 RULE OF BUSINESS

Whenever you find yourself experiencing a slow month (30 days), look back 90 days on your calendar to find the cause.

Years ago, I taught the 7-Touch Rule to marketing in which you can expect to present an offer to a warm contact at least 7 times before they'd buy. Additionally, I referenced the 20-Step Guide to Advertising in which you have to advertise to a cold contact up to 20 times before they're interested. A warm contact is someone who knows and trusts you already, and a cold contact is someone who's just finding you for the first time—no trust established.

Those rules have radically changed in a short period of time. With social media, you're bombarded with sales messages in a most personal way and at every turn. Therefore, it typically takes as many as 20 touches before a warm contact buys, and as many as 50 (!) introductions before a cold contact takes interest.

And that's why what you were doing 90 days ago effects the 30 days you are experiencing now. This June, I enjoyed a phenomenal period of new sales and sign-ups, which is random and unusual for summer. Looking back 90 days, it all made sense. I ran an experiment three months before: I amped up my output (marketing 5x my normal shares on social). I was everywhere all the time, and because of that, people who found me then were buying from me 90 days later.

Likewise, I experienced an incredible sales slump on the 2017 edition of *Your Best Year*. It sold less than its predecessor (*Your Best Year 2016*) which made absolutely no sense because it was better and already had an enormous fan base. For months, I struggled to make sense of it ... until I considered the 30-90 Rule.

Every year for the launch of *Your Best Year*, I blog about it for months starting in October. Only, last year I didn't. Instead, I moved houses and took much-needed time off to help my family readjust and recover from the transition.

When I was experiencing slow sales in January, it wasn't because of what I was doing in January. The book's popularity suffered because of what I'd failed to do in October.

That's why it is so important to keep your goals front and center, work ahead toward the big picture, and never let a slump slow you down. Otherwise, its effect will hit you twice—now and again in 90 days!

Look back on your first annual strategy (page 63), and apply the 30-90 Rule to your promotions. How can you amp up your output 90 days before big promotions to ensure buyers will be all the more engaged when you launch your moneymakers? Add that in!

7 STEPS TO PROFIT BREAKTHROUGH

These are the seven steps I took to outgrow my limitations and conquer my fears at every stage of the game. Some of this material is a summary of concepts you have learned in this book.

#1 Trust the Business to Provide

In order to achieve the next level in my business, I know I need to trust my business to provide and barrel-roll through my goals. There can be no pumping of the breaks, doubting my abilities, or second-guessing the direction I'm headed.

I stopped him-hawing on trivial decisions in both personal life and work, such as "Should I buy that book? Should I upgrade my phone? Should I invest in more business training?"

Don't *hope* you'll hit your target, barrel-roll through it. There's no room for uncertainty, and there's no time for hesitation.

> The $30K me: Worked on a shoe-string budget and collected profits without trusting, or even thinking about, long-term gain. I didn't rely on the income at all, and only used the funds for extra spending money.
>
> The $250K me: Set monthly income goals, and took responsibility for personal expenses. I bought myself my first brand new car and hired an assistant before I hit the six-figure mark. These commitments stretched my financial comfort zone, but it also forced me to become a true professional.
>
> The $1M me: Unabashedly invests in myself (in both personal and professional aspects). I make risky decisions that 98% of online business owners avoid, such as hiring full-time support, signing contracts with world-class professionals, and publicly sharing income reports.

#2 Build Confidence

Outward appearances matter, just not as much as we think they do in the beginning.

When I set out to increase my income, I thought I needed a better website to make it happen. (I didn't.) My web design had always been make do: a WordPress template and a graphic designer I found online. The cheap contracts cost way more than they were worth in frustration, broken things I never knew how to fix, and overall jankiness.

I cleaned up what I could and saved up for what I wanted. Along the way, I presented myself as if I already had the professional appearance I craved.

The newly redesigned Marketing Creativity™ is a daily reminder that I said, "Yes! I believe," to my career, talents, and abilities. It displays all of my hard work so beautifully and showcases my expertise so efficiently.

> The $30K me: Worried myself into a rut. I didn't feel recognized enough to make my work known, and I deeply resented people with over-the-top false confidence.
>
> The $250K me: Studied those jokers with false confidence! You know who I mean: they're louder, less informed, overrated, and less qualified, but they act as though they're the leader of the free world. I realized that presenting myself with confidence was an area of weakness, and I was so resentful because it's sometimes a strength in the lesser qualified.
>
> The $1M me: Knows my worth as a service provider and your worth as a client. I deeply value us both, and I confidently help tens of thousands of online business owners on a daily basis.

#3 Hire Pros

This goes hand in hand with building confidence, and comes up again in step four. Your network online and the people you surround yourself with in real life matter way more than you realize.

> The $30K me: Built a jerry-rigged system, used bulky membership plug-ins, and signed up for an "affordable" email management.
>
> The $250K me: Developed a stream-lined, automated system, bought a powerful membership software, hired a full-time assistant and on-call support staff, signed up for customer relationship management, and bought the least janky webinar software money can buy (none have been excellent). I also hired tax professionals, but continued to DIY photography and bookkeeping.
>
> The $1M me: Has custom-built everything. I hired the best designer, developer, lawyer, and bookkeeper. I retained the best assistant. I'll soon have self-hosted opt-ins and sales sequences, and I'm fearlessly chasing more upgrades.

#4 Value Your Time

When I say "value your time," I mean, DEEPLY VALUE YOUR TIME in all caps; I'm begging from the bottom of my heart.

Don't let people call you during your work hours and drone on and on because they're bored at their job. Don't let text messages interrupt your day just because they know you're home. Don't let people guilt-trip or depend on you for their happiness. And please, for the love of the living, excuse yourself from toxic relationships right this minute.

I found it utterly impossible to build my self-esteem while core relationships in my life seemed determined to tear it down. I started to pay close attention to my conversations about success in business. If I felt the need to "soften the blow" of my good news because the person I told would be threatened by it, I recognized that person as an emotional vampire.

> The $30K me: Answered the phone on-call for friends and family (during their bus rides, breaks at work, daily commutes, lunch hours, etc.). They knew I was laying the bricks of my business, but I was "too polite" to tell them I could not be disturbed. I was involved with toxic relationships in which I didn't feel safe enough to share even the smallest of wins. The success I did share was either ignored or excused as fluke circumstance. During this period, one relative sarcastically said in jest, "Oh yeah, you're going to make *a million dollars*." True story.
>
> The $250K me: Let everyone know I was not to be disturbed during work hours. Period. I changed my home phone and refused to give out the new number—that was my "office" line. My response to the kickback I received: "I don't call you at work, so don't call me there, either." My boundaries were met with resistance and confusion. I stopped "softening the blow" when discussing my success. I no longer sought validation and approval outside of myself. Toxic relationships were suffocated and/or banned.
>
> The $1M me: Loves investing in relationships that are genuine and authentic. I enjoy meeting new people. New people serve as a reminder that I have, in my home, the very best people on the planet (my husband and children). My focus is them, and the rest is just a bonus. I'm thankful that the people we let into our circle add value and friendship to the clean, healthy energy we create.

"THE WOMAN WHO DOES NOT REQUIRE VALIDATION FROM ANYONE IS THE MOST FEARED INDIVIDUAL ON THE PLANET."—*Mohadesa Najumi*

#5 Don't Give Your Power Away

As I was finding success in business, a reality series about entrepreneur, Jillian Michaels aired on TV. She's a force to be reckoned with, and in many of her dealings, Jillian threatens the room with a metaphorical bazooka.

What I've learned since then is that, when it comes to business, there is always a bazooka in the room. The bazooka represents the power, so if you want to succeed, you better make sure it's in your corner. And if anybody's going to wield it during a transaction, it has to be you.

One thing I've really paid attention to in this last year is: When my power escapes me, how did I lose it and whom did I give it to? At first, I was scared that owning my power meant losing my softness, that I would somehow be harder. I was literally shaking the first time I picked up the bazooka in a meeting, but I came away with the control and the respect I deserved in the situation.

The $30K me: Sought constant validation and approval outside of myself, waited for some ambiguous "big break" to come along and prove my worth, looked to gatekeepers (traditional book publishers, Etsy editors, WordPress spotlights, etc.) in hopes of being featured or recognized.

The $250K me: Said, "screw that!" to all of the above. I made a name for myself by myself, single-handedly claimed best-seller status on Amazon, took my talents to CreativeLive (I've taught four courses there so far), unabashedly self-promoted, and sold my high-quality, high-value membership and courses like a boss.

The $1M me: Looks for opportunities to strengthen my power, and I welcome every new challenge that tests my boundaries. This year, I'll show up more in every way: on camera, in person, for my dreams, in my career. I relentlessly pursue excellence.

#6 Honor Your Talent

As mentioned earlier, I liken my business to a doctor's practice. Imagine an experienced physician—studied, trained, and skilled—answering her own phones, recording new patient information, monitoring each person's blood pressure and temperature, taking her own notes and records, and doing the billing at the end of each appointment.

Would you respect her expertise more or less for it?

How about if you had her email address and felt entitled to ask questions, send comments, and make requests on demand? Just because you're in online business does not mean you need to have an open-email policy. Professionals need to set boundaries and reserve their time and energy for paying clients.

The $30K me: Did everything, all at once with zero boundaries. My family could never tell if I was working (or just browsing the internet) because I was on the computer always.

The $250K me: Created a working schedule and policies for myself and my business.

The $1M me: Works with a dedicated team of professionals to ensure I'm always in my zone of genius (content, marketing, and planning).

#7 Marketing is the Name of the Game

Nothing online matters unless people stick to it, and this is something I discuss regularly with online stat-lovers! They say,

"Yes! My views are up!"
"Oh no, my views are down!"
"I'm not getting any views! What's going on?!!"

If you asked my stat-loving readers, views are the new currency … only, they're worth nothing. Views without sales mean the storefront's not doing its job, which is to sell a product. Views without subscribers mean the website's not doing its job, which is to connect with like-minded customers.

That said, let's talk about what really matters—how to make your visitors stick and convert. There are a few things you'll want to always be working on if you're looking to build an online business:

- An email list (it's king)
- Photography (it's queen)
- Copywriting (it fills the royal court)

The definitions of "marketing" are terrible. I love the act of marketing, and I hate every single way it's defined. Except for this sentence, which I found on Wikipedia after a lot of dull and monotonous words …

"Marketing is used to create the customer, to keep the customer, and to satisfy the customer."

Marketing is everything that involves the customer. Its definition should be, "the act or instance of doing business." If a thriving business is what you want to have, then marketing is what you need to do. Simply put, if your business isn't exceeding your expectations, then marketing is the missing link.

> <u>The $30K me</u>: Checked stats, cared about views, and was deeply aware of vanity metrics (number of followers, social media engagement, etc.).
>
> <u>The $250K me</u>: Recorded financial gains daily, used social media to increase my reach (rather than be used by it), and paid attention to the numbers that mattered (email subscribers and sales conversions).
>
> <u>The $1M me</u>: Aggressively shares my work with the world to improve lives and create a ripple effect of better.

I believe in empowering creatives to do work they love and profit greatly from it. I aim to help people add more LIFE! into their lives to make their days better, which in effect, makes their customer's days better, their children's days better, their partner's days better …

And you can do the same!

RECOMMENDATION LIST

These beautiful people, books, and resources made my year a whole lot better.

- *Marketing Playbook: How to Scale Your Online Business to Outrageous Success* by Lisa Jacobs
- *How Bad Do You Want It? Mastering the Psychology of Mind Over Muscle* by Matt Fitzgerald
- *Deep Survival: Who Lives, Who Dies, and Why* by Laurence Gonzales
- Jennie Rensink—project manager, business operations extraordinaire
- Kara Benz—dear friend, supporter, and planner extraordinaire
- *Pitch Anything: An Innovative Method for Presenting, Persuading, and Winning the Deal* by Oren Klaff—a brilliant book to teach you how to build confidence and take control
- Grit & Wit—the designer behind my gorgeous new website
- Denise Duffield-Thomas—author of *Get Rich, Lucky Bitch!* and Money Bootcamp
- Ramit Sethi—author of *I Will Teach You to Be Rich* and Growth Lab
- Mel Robbins—author of *The 5 Second Rule* and the Power of You course
- Exquiture Web Development
- Christina Scalera—my friend and lawyer
- Paige French Photography—my friend and photographer
- John Rensink—My assistant Jennie's husband and my bookkeeper
- *The Twelve Week Year: Get More Done in 12 Weeks than Others Do in 12 Months* by Brian P. Moran and Michael Lennington
- *Compound Effect: Jumpstart Your Income, Your Life, Your Success* by Darren Hardy
- Netflix Original Documentary—*Tony Robbins: I am not your Guru*
- *Against All Grain: Delectable Paleo Recipes to Eat Well and Feel Great* by Danielle Walker
- *Making Life Easy: A Simple Guide to a Divinely Inspired Life* by Christiane Northrup M.D.
- CreativeLive—favorite instructors include Bonnie Christine, Sue Bryce, and Mel Robbins
- *The One Thing: The Surprisingly Simple Truth Behind Extraordinary Results* by Gary W. Keller and Jay Papasan
- *Unshakeable: Your Financial Freedom Playbook* by Tony Robins
- Louise L. Hay, with so much gratitude and love
- Tim Ferris—more specifically, exercises and resources from *Tools of Titans*
- Postcron—the low-cost social media scheduler that does it all
- Facebook Live Video for webcasts

ABOUT LISA JACOBS

In case we are just meeting, I'm Lisa Jacobs, a marketing strategist and blogger. During my 10-year career, I've built and succeeded at two different types of businesses. The first was a product-based online store, the Energy Shop. I marketed the shop to sold-out success, and during its run, it was in the top 2% of highest earning storefronts on Etsy.

The second is my service-based business and blog, Marketing Creativity™. I offer marketing strategy in the form of books, online courses, and private consultations. My revenue exceeds a quarter of a million dollars annually, putting me in the top 8% of highest earning websites on the internet.

I'm Lisa Jacobs, and I help inspired entrepreneurs showcase their talents, strengthen their weaknesses, and market their creativity.

This book is my art. It is a painting I've been working on my entire life, and each year it gains more detail: better focus and enhanced clarity. I love self-discovery, strategic growth, and measured results, and because I love it so, I'm honored to be part of your journey.

I call you a "creative" entrepreneur, but I get a lot of kickback on that from people who don't identify as creative. The thing is, by blazing your own trail, you are creating: a product, a brand, a name for yourself, a business, a client base, an audience, and a unique vision of success.

You are creative. And brave. And interesting. And powerful.

The goals you have set for yourself with this workbook are what's required for your personal vision of success. The journey ahead of you is not the easiest choice, I assure you. I applaud your commitment and thank you for your courage and service! Your passion makes the whole world come more alive.

This year, do things differently. Make bold choices and demolish the foundation of your comfort zone. Be interesting. Accomplish something that makes you unabashedly proud of yourself and then go brag about it. Come alive in your skin because you're made of energy. BE THAT LIFE. Create with it and let it flow through you without filter. I'll root for you every step of the way.

If you should need me, find me in my zone — talking shop and strategizing growth at marketyourcreativity.com. Be sure to share your results and cozy planning days with me using #yby2018. Here's to your best year yet.